INTERNATIONAL SERIES OF MONOGRAPHS IN
EXPERIMENTAL PSYCHOLOGY

GENERAL EDITOR: H. J. EYSENCK

VOLUME 18

PERSONALITY DIFFERENCES AND BIOLOGICAL VARIATIONS: A STUDY OF TWINS

OTHER TITLES IN THE SERIES IN EXPERIMENTAL PSYCHOLOGY

PERSONALITY DIFFERENCES AND BIOLOGICAL VARIATIONS: A STUDY OF TWINS

BY

GORDON CLARIDGE
SANDRA CANTER
and
W. I. HUME

PERGAMON PRESS

OXFORD · NEW YORK · TORONTO
SYDNEY · BRAUNSCHWEIG

Pergamon Press Ltd., Headington Hill Hall, Oxford

Pergamon Press Inc., Maxwell House, Fairview Park, Elmsford, New York 10523

Pergamon of Canada Ltd., 207 Queen's Quay West, Toronto 1

Pergamon Press (Aust.) Pty. Ltd., 19a Boundary Street, Rushcutters Bay, N.S.W. 2011, Australia

Vieweg & Sohn GmbH, Burgplatz 1, Braunschweig

First edition 1973

Library of Congress Cataloging in Publication Data

Claridge, Gordon S
Personality differences and biological variations.

(International series of monographs in experimental psychology, v. 18)
1. Twins.   2.   Individuality.   3.   Variation
(Biology) I.   Canter, Sandra.   II.   Hume, Wilfred I.
III.   Title.   [DNLM: 1.   Genetics, Human.
2.   Personality.   3.   Twins.   W1 IN835K v. 18 1973,
XNLM: [GN 265.M8 C591p   1973]]
BF723.T9C58   1973   155.2'2   72–10132
ISBN 0–08–017124–9

Printed in Great Britain by A. Wheaton & Co., Exeter

CONTENTS

v

194154

PREFACE

IT is not often that psychologists find themselves in the position of having obtained their sample of subjects before they have designed their experiment. Normally, for all but the most creative, this might be an embarrassing predicament. But when the subjects are twins, their availability seems to come almost as a gift from the gods. The gods in our case were Dr Watson Buchanan and his colleagues at the Glasgow Centre for Rheumatic Diseases. Some eight years ago Dr Buchanan rang our department to ask if we were interested in taking over a twin register they had formed during a research project they themselves had just completed. What scientist worth his salt could resist such an offer! As biologically orientated psychologists my colleagues and I were naturally interested in the genetic aspects of behaviour and the ready availability of a "captive" sample of twins removed one of our excuses for not having researched in the area before. Even at that time, however, we were aware of the disadvantages of embarking on a large-scale twin project. For one thing it would entail a massive diversion of research effort away from our main lines of enquiry into psychiatric disorder. We also knew that it would be all too easy to tramp yet again over some already well-trodden ground, an exercise whose aimlessness was nicely summed up recently by Dr Lyndon Eaves in a psycho-genetics symposium at the British Psychological Society's 1971 London Conference, when he said of conventional twin studies that "all they contribute are more statistically significant entries to an ever expanding list of heritability estimates based on small samples of twins". In planning the present investigation, therefore, we deliberately tried to avoid the pitfalls of aim and interpretation that bedevil many experiments carried out within the "classic" twin design; attempting a study which was not focused narrowly on the genetics of behaviour but which was concerned with the biological basis of individual differences in its broadest sense. To this end we undertook a series of interlocking experiments which could be linked theoretically to other parallel studies being carried out in the rest of our research programme. We hope that

vii

we have managed to achieve some of the objectives we had in view eight years ago.

Inevitably, once we had made contact with our twin sample, other ideas for research occurred to us and further experiments begun. In addition, several workers elsewhere expressed interest in gaining access to our twin register in order to carry out studies of their own, or to reanalyse our data from a different point of view. This book therefore covers only part of the data collected on the twin sample. To have included more would, we felt, have detracted from its main theme and made it lose theoretical coherence. Publication of the book would also have been delayed even further than it has already. However, some readers may be interested in the results of other work that was done with the twins and for their benefit we have included in a short appendix a list of the various research areas studied and the names and addresses of investigators from whom further details may be obtained. Enquiries from *prospective* researchers wanting access to the twin register might be less welcome, at least by the twins themselves, whose patience has already been sorely tried!

Indeed, it is to the twins that our first acknowledgement of help must go for responding with typical Scots generosity and good-humour to the persistent demands made on them by three dour Sassenach investigators. Payment of the twins' expenses was made from a grant (No. ACMR 689) provided by the Advisory Committee on Medical Research of the Scottish Home and Health Department, whose assistance in this respect is acknowledged. For organizing and carrying out the procedures involved in determining the zygosity of the twins, grateful thanks are due to Professor J. Renwick, formerly of the Glasgow University Institute of Genetics, and to Dr Andrew Pollock, formerly of the Department of Haematology, Southern General Hospital, Glasgow. Also at the Southern General Hospital Mr Louden Brown and his colleagues of the Department of Medical Illustration there prepared the figures for the book to their usual high standards.

Finally, as senior author and prefator of the book I must record my thanks to my two colleagues for carrying out much of the donkey work during data collection; as I am sure they will wish to acknowledge my own efficiency in editing *and* typing the manuscript so expertly.

Glasgow   GORDON CLARIDGE

CHAPTER 1

INTRODUCTION TO THE TWIN PROJECT

By GORDON CLARIDGE

The aims of the project

It is natural to suppose that, given access as we were to a large sample of human twins, the main purpose in studying them would be to exploit their genetic uniqueness, collecting information on them which might throw light on the influence of heredity on certain defined characteristics, in our case behavioural and psychological characteristics. And indeed this was an important aim of the various studies brought together in the following chapters. However, none of the contributors to this book is a geneticist, nor even a psychologist particularly specialized in that branch of genetics, namely behaviour genetics or psychogenetics, which is most relevant to psychology. As experimental psychopathologists we have been primarily concerned with establishing the scientific principles of personality, using a wide range of objective behavioural and physiological techniques. Most of our previous research on the problem has been focused on the abnormalities of behaviour observed in psychiatric patients (see Claridge, 1967). However, it is an assumption of our approach to personality that the characteristics observed and measured in the psychiatrically ill are merely exaggerated forms of those found running through the general population. The ready availability of a substantial number of psychiatrically well adults therefore allowed us to extend our research to the study of the normal personality, thus giving the project a second major purpose, namely the investigation of behaviour *per se*, irrespective of our subjects being twins.

1

Of course, these two aims are closely intertwined, especially so in this instance. For, as will be discussed in more detail later, the particular theoretical approach to personality adopted here lays great emphasis on the biological basis of behaviour. As such it tends naturally to seek evidence for the genetic determinants of personality; so it was of considerable interest to us to compare our twins for their resemblance (or otherwise) on the parameters we chose to study.

When looking at our data from the genetic viewpoint we mainly used, because of the nature of our sample, the "classic" twin method, the rationale of which derives from the existence of two types of twin: one-egg, monozygotic, or MZ, and two-egg, dizygotic, or DZ, twins. The method involves comparing the two types of twin for their relative similarity on a chosen characteristic. If the characteristic has a significant hereditary component, then MZ twins, being genetically identical, should be more alike than DZ twins. DZ twins will also be alike but no more so than ordinary brothers or sisters. Although widely used in genetic investigations the twin method has been subjected to criticism and some comment is necessary on its value as a research strategy in behavioural genetics.

The twin method

A major criticism of the classic twin method concerns its assumption that the environment exerts a similar influence on the two types of twin being compared. Thus, if samples of MZ twins prove to be significantly more alike than comparable samples of DZ twins on a particular characteristic, the method assumes that the greater resemblance of the former is due entirely to their identical genetic make-up, the effects of the environment on the characteristic having been held constant. However, against this it has commonly been argued that because they *are* genetically identical, MZ twins will be exposed to a more similar environment than DZ twins; for example, through MZ pairs forming closer attachments to each other than DZ pairs (Shields, 1954) or being treated more alike by their parents (Jones, 1955). This criticism of the twin method has naturally been directed particularly at studies of psychological characteristics, such as personality traits, and at first glance it might seem less pertinent to investigations involving biological or physiological parameters, a number of which were included in the present project. However, even there the logic of assuming equal environments in twins has been questioned. Thus, Lilienfeld (1961), quoting the fact that serum cholesterol levels are more alike in MZ than in DZ twins, argues that the result does not necessarily prove genetic control of the characteristic but may simply indicate that dietary or other environmental factors which influence serum cholesterol are more similar in MZ twins.

The "hen or egg" nature of the problem is well illustrated in the arguments put forward by two investigators who have recently examined environmental bias in twin studies and who have reached opposite conclusions. Smith (1965) interviewed adolescent twins about their personal and social activities, such as dress and study habits, sports and other leisure pursuits, and food preferences. He found that in general the home environments of MZ co-twins were more alike than those of DZ co-twins, particularly so in the case of female pairs. He concluded that the results throw considerable doubt on the validity of assuming equal environments in twin research.

On the other hand, Scarr (1968), who in a comparable study found similar results, suggests that as they stand such data do not provide evidence either for or against the existence of environmental bias in heritability estimates. She points out that, while the results obtained by Smith and herself could certainly arise because of more powerful environmental pressures for similarity in MZ twins, at the same time the latter could be more alike because their genotypic identity itself leads to more similar parental treatment and hence to greater behavioural resemblance. Scarr argues that a crucial test of these two possibilities is the comparison of MZ and DZ pairs subdivided according to whether their parents have correctly identified the zygosity of their twin children. Re-analysing her own data from this point of view, Scarr found that it was the *actual* genetic relatedness of twins, rather than the parents' belief about their zygosity, which determined parental treatment. Thus, mothers who wrongly believed their MZ twins to be DZ nevertheless frequently treated them like correctly identified MZ pairs and similarly for mothers who wrongly judged their DZ twins to be MZ. Scarr concludes that the kind of parental treatment twins receive is itself an expression of the original genotypic similarity or dissimilarity and that the case for environmental bias in twin research has been overstated. Although the present writer is not entirely convinced that Scarr's line of reasoning really answers the criticism that twin studies tend to over-estimate the contribution of heredity, her results do illustrate the complexity of the problem.

Of course, it is possible to minimize error due to environmental bias by studying twins who have been reared apart from birth. Similarities observed among MZ twins can then be less easily explained as being due to their having had a common environment. However, such studies are difficult to carry out because of the rarity of known separated twin pairs. When they have been undertaken some surprising results, relevant to the issue under discussion, have emerged. Thus, Shields (1962) found for the personality trait of extraversion that separated twins were actually somewhat *more* alike than twins brought up to-gether. The implication of this finding is that when reared in close contact with each other the members of a twin pair seek to establish independent identities by developing complementary roles that exag-gerate the differences, rather than the similarities, between them. Freed from the restraint of having a genetically related, and sometimes physically identical, sibling of the same age, the individual reared apart from his twin may be able to develop characteristics closer to his geno-type. Although anticipating somewhat, it is worth noting that results obtained in the present study, while based on data of a slightly different kind, have led us to reach a similar conclusion (see Chapter 2).

The point is that environmental bias need not necessarily lead to overestimation of the genetic contribution to a particular characteristic. Naturally it is error in that direction which has been focused upon by those critics of the twin method who have a preference for environmental, rather than genetic, explanations of behaviour. However, an equally strong, or at least a no less weak, case can be made for the view that heritability estimates based on twin data are often *underestimates*. For it can be argued that from fertilization onwards the biological pressures, at least on MZ twins, is towards relative dissimilarity compared with DZ twins. In general it would seem that the embryological division to produce "identical" twin individuals is itself a potentially asymmetric process (Darlington, 1954) and possibly even an abnormal one (Bulmer,

1970). Thus, the latter author discusses experimental evidence from lower animals showing that developmental retardation at a very early stage, caused by factors such as oxygen lack, can actually produce monozygotic twinning. He suggests some connection between this fact and the observation that congenital abnormalities are much more frequent in MZ twins compared with single births, though the incidence in DZ pairs is not increased. Furthermore, the pre-natal environment as a whole may be more different for some MZ pairs than it is for DZ pairs because of the imbalance of placental circulation found in those MZ twins—about two-thirds—who are monochorial.

On the whole, therefore, it would seem that environmental pressures on monozygotic twins are not uniform in their direction, some leading to relative discordance and others tending to capitalize on existing genetic similarities. It would be tempting to conclude that these two sources of error in estimating genotypic resemblance would cancel out. However, that would be a naïve assumption since the direction of environmental bias will clearly depend both on the kind of characteristic studied and on the stage at which non-genetic factors exert their influence. Nor would it be feasible to distinguish clearly in this respect between biological and behavioural characteristics, arguing that the former might be more sensitive to intra-uterine effects which lead to dissimilarity and the latter to post-natal effects leading to similarity. For not only will behaviour subtly reflect pre-natally influenced biological differences between monozygotic pairs, but, in addition, as the results on separated twins quoted above illustrate, the post-natal environment may act directly on behaviour to produce phenotypic dissimilarity, rather than similarity, in MZ twins.

From what has been said it is clear that the simple comparison of unseparated MZ and DZ twins cannot yield precise estimates of the relative influence of genetic and environmental factors on multi-determined characteristics of the kind studied here. Nor can it specify the mode of inheritance of such characteristics. To do that it is necessary to carry out more complete family studies, looking at correlations between relatives other than twins and applying complex statistical procedures like the Multiple Abstract Variance Analysis (MAVA) described by Cattell (1965) or the techniques of biometrical genetics developed by Fisher (1918) and later by Mather (1949) and extensively applied recently to human traits by Jinks and his colleagues (Jinks and Fulker, 1970).†

This is not to say that the classic twin method is valueless. Indeed, as Mittler (1971) implies in a recent review of the method, it may be extremely useful if one proceeds with an eye to its limitations, refusing to enter sterile and simplistic nature/nurture controversies and recognizing that twin research is directed as much towards throwing light on environmental influences in behaviour as it is towards elucidating genetic factors. Admittedly it is the latter that has been the usual motive for carrying out twin studies in the past, the main emphasis being on the search for similarity or concordance across groups of twins. However, looked at in a different way, twin data can often provide useful information about the role of specific environmental factors in behaviour. This alternative approach involves focusing on twin *differences* rather than similarities, examining MZ pairs who, despite being genetically identical, differ markedly on some characteristic and then looking for other correlated variations which might explain why such twins are discordant. This method has been applied to behavioural traits by Brown *et al.* (1967) and by a number of workers to MZ pairs discordant for psychosomatic illnesses (Pilot *et al.*, 1963; Greene and Swisher, 1969) and psychiatric disorder (Mosher *et al.*, 1971; MacSweeney, 1970). Some examples of this approach taken from our own data are described later in Chapters 5 and 7.

In planning the present project, then, it was recognized that from a genetic point of view its main value would lie in enabling us to sift out parameters of behaviour which appeared to have a significant hereditary component and which could then, if necessary, be studied in detail using the more precise genetic techniques referred to earlier. In some cases particular measurements, such as the sedation threshold described in Chapter 5, had never previously been studied in twins and its investigation from a genetic viewpoint was of unique interest. Other measures, of

† Although successful application of the model-fitting procedures involved in biometrical genetics requires more extensive kinship data than that provided by the conventional twin study, it is worth recording that the measures used in the present investigation were, as an exercise, subjected to biometrical genetical analysis by Dr Lyndon Eaves of the Department of Genetics at the University of Birmingham. The results of that analysis are not reported in this book, but any interested reader can obtain further details by writing to either Dr Eaves or the present author.

course, particularly those of personality and cognitive function, had already been the subject of twin research, though rarely had they formed part of a larger battery of psychological and psychophysiological tests given to the same individuals. The inclusion here of a wide range of variables meant that it was possible, where appropriate, to cross-correlate measurements taken at different levels of behaviour. This had two advantages. First, it provided a broad set of data against which to assess the results of comparing twins on single parameters. Secondly, it fulfilled the other main aim of the project, namely the extension of our work on psychiatric patients to the study of individual variations among normal subjects. The theoretical framework within which the study as a whole was planned is discussed further in the next section.

Theoretical background of the project

Since a wide range of cognitive, personality, and physiological variables was involved in the present study it would be absurd to pretend that they were all selected and investigated from a single theoretical viewpoint. In some cases individual tests were chosen for reasons that were very largely empirical, often because it was simply considered of interest to study them in relation to other procedures that had been studied. However, the principal theme of our investigation was the analysis of personality within a biological framework and more particularly that of "nervous typology". The latter theory regards observable personality differences as being partly due to individual variations in the way in which central nervous processes are organized. This essentially Pavlovian view of personality has found theoretical expression in various forms in contemporary psychology, both among Russian workers (Gray, 1964) and in the West (Eysenck, 1967; Claridge, 1967). While there are still some disagreements about which is the most appropriate nervous typological model for conceptualizing and analysing personality variation, the differences that exist among workers in the field are ones of emphasis rather than of principle. All would tend to agree that personality can be usefully seen as being organized in an essentially hierarchical fashion. Thus, at the "descriptive" level personality can be viewed in terms of traits or broad dimensions of behaviour, such as extraversion or anxiety, these being mainly, though as discussed later not exclusively, measurable with questionnaire techniques. At a second, biological, level these observable characteristics can be linked to nervous typological variations, measured with a wide range of techniques derived from psychophysiology and experimental psychology (Claridge, 1970).

The very nature of the theoretical approach just described inevitably means that it focuses attention particularly on the constitutional determinants of personality. Indeed, the most formally stated of the nervous typological theories, that of Eysenck (1960), makes explicit reference, in discussing the stratified organization of the personality, to its "phenotypic" (descriptive) and "genotypic" (causal) levels. This does not mean, as far as the present investigators were concerned, that we were committed at the outset to any particular viewpoint about the role of heredity in personality. With respect to that issue we are simply interested in using nervous typological theory as a vehicle for exploring the processes whereby genetic and environmental factors interact at different levels of behaviour to produce individual differences in personality. In doing so the only, rather broad, expectation we had was that hereditary influences would probably reveal themselves more clearly and be relatively more important at the psychophysiological, than at the descriptive, level of personality.

As far as the particular nervous typological model adopted here is concerned, we were guided in our selection of measures and our analysis of the data by the personality theory developed by Claridge (1967). This does not mean that the contributors to the project—apart from the present author!—were in any sense committed to the theory. Indeed, as will be clear in the following chapters, the analysis of individual sets of data, such as questionnaire measures, was carried out without reference to any particular theory. However, the model was of value when we came to cross-correlate measures from different parts of the study. A considerable amount and a great variety of data were collected on the twin sample and it would have been tempting to inter-correlate, and perhaps factor analyse, all of the measures available in the hope that theoretically meaningful results would emerge. However, it is our experience that the usual outcome of such exercises in computer madness is numerical gibberish. We chose instead, therefore, to adopt a more systematic, if more limited, approach, namely an examination of those relationships within the data which could test out specific hypotheses derived from the present author's previous work on the psychophysiological basis of personality. The latter's nervous typological model was originally developed out of Eysenck's, but subsequently took a different course and now departs from it in a number of important ways.

First, compared with Eysenck's theory, it has been less exclusively directed towards establishing the nervous typological basis of extraversion in normal people. Instead, it has concentrated more on the study of psychiatric patients, using the latter as criterion groups for isolating psychophysiological rather than descriptive dimensions which can account for differences in normal and abnormal personality. Secondly, it has placed greater emphasis on the psychotic reactions as conditions which can define important sources of variation in normal personality. Thirdly, and perhaps most important of all, the way in which nervous typological organization is related to personality at the descriptive level is conceptualized differently. Eysenck, starting from his orthogonal dimensional structure of personality, has postulated that underlying each dimension is a distinct and functionally independent psychophysiological mechanism. Thus, in the latest version of his theory (Eysenck, 1967) he suggests that variations in arousal and activation form the basis, respectively, of extraversion and neuroticism. The model used here, on the other hand, starts from the causal end and proposes that it is differences in the *interaction* between the same set of nervous typological processes that are the crucial characteristics distinguishing different personality dimensions. The problem for research in the area is therefore seen to be one of discovering the varieties of nervous typological organization rather than that of specifying the particular causal process which is separately responsible for each personality dimension.

The actual details of the model adopted here are more appropriately described in a later chapter (Chapter 6) where it is used as a basis for integrating the different kinds of data obtained in the twin study. In the meantime, however, a more general point should be made about its influence on the choice of measures investigated in our twin sample. As mentioned above, our previous research has been very much concerned with the study of psychosis and psychoticism within a nervous typological framework. This has involved looking at the relationship between psychophysiological parameters and behavioural variables which, at the descriptive level, might reflect important features of psychoticism. Particularly important in this context are cognitive tests, especially those regarded as measures of "thinking style" or studied under headings like "overinclusion". It was therefore considerations of this kind that led to the choice of cognitive variables discussed in Chapter 3. One consequence of including such variables is a widening of what are considered to be appropriate measures of the descriptive level of personality. As used by Eysenck the latter refers mainly to those aspects of behaviour that are measured by personality questionnaires. However, it would seem legitimate to extend to other sources of individual variation, not usually considered as falling in the personality sphere, the same hierarchical notions inherent in nervous typological theory. Admittedly, in the case of cognitive functions the link between the psychophysiological and descriptive levels of behaviour is as yet more tenuous and based mainly on the study of psychotic patients (e.g. see Claridge, 1967). Nevertheless, further examination of the problem would seem well worthwhile, the present study providing an ideal opportunity to carry out such an investigation.

The twin sample

Selection and description of the sample

As acknowledged in the preface to this book, the stimulus to carry out the present study came from the ready availability of a sample of twins collected by another group of workers in the City of Glasgow. Their original sample was obtained by personal contact and by advertising in the local hospitals and in the press. From the list of names they supplied we selected all adult pairs of the same sex aged between 16 and 55 years. The twins were then contacted by post and asked if they would be willing to participate in the project, the nature of which was fully explained to them. Those who volunteered formed the main nucleus of the final sample, which was later increased in size by getting a local newspaper to run a story on the project asking for further twins who were interested in taking part. This was necessary because at the halfway stage in the study we discovered that we had a relative shortage of male dizygotic pairs. The response to the newspaper appeal was enormous—embarrassingly so—because the locally released story spread to the national, and international, press. Of the several hundred pairs of twins who volunteered we selected those who met our criterion for inclusion and who were within easy reach of our laboratory. Of the total group of twins the majority came from Glasgow or its surrounding area, though some were resident in other parts of Scotland including, in one case, the Isle of Lewis. Occasionally, when one member of a pair lived elsewhere, say in England, the opportunity of testing the exiled twin was taken when he or she returned on a visit to Glasgow.

Because of the large quantity of information collected on the twins it was not possible, for one reason or another, to obtain a complete set of data for all pairs. The sample sizes, therefore, varied slightly for different measures or groups of measure and these details are presented in the appropriate chapters. However, the total group that we drew upon consisted of ninety-five pairs of twins. Forty-four of these were judged to be MZ and fifty-one DZ, the actual method for determining zygosity being described in the next section. In selecting the two types of twin we tried as far as possible to match the MZ and DZ samples on five variables: sex, age, social class, intelligence, and length of separation. The results of this matching are shown in Tables 1.1–1.5.

TABLE 1.1
TWIN SAMPLE BACKGROUND DATA
SEX

	Male	Female
MZ twins (44 pairs)	23%	77%
DZ twins (51 pairs)	27%	73%

With regard to sex distribution it can be seen from Table 1.1 that the MZ and DZ samples were well matched, but that in both groups there was a disproportionate number of females: over 70% in fact. Table 1.2 shows the age distribution. Again there was fairly good matching across the two groups, but an overall preponderance of individuals in the age range 16–25 years. Social class (Table 1.3) also showed a somewhat

TABLE 1.2
TWIN SAMPLE BACKGROUND DATA
AGE

	16–25	26–35	36–45	46–55
MZ twins (44 pairs)	57%	25%	16%	2%
DZ twins (51 pairs)	62%	20%	12%	6%

skewed distribution, 80% of the twins in both groups coming from Social Class 3 or above. Matching here was fairly close, though slightly more of the MZ twins fell into Social Class 1. With regard to intelligence, which is given in terms of Progressive Matrices grade (Table 1.4), there

TABLE 1.3
TWIN SAMPLE BACKGROUND DATA
SOCIAL CLASS

	1	2	3	4	5
MZ twins (44 pairs)	11%	23%	48%	11%	7%
DZ twins (51 pairs)	4%	29%	47%	10%	10%

was again good matching but an overall tendency for the distribution to be skewed. Thus, over 70% of the MZ and nearly 60% of the DZ twins obtained Matrices grades of either I or II. Finally, Table 1.5 compares

TABLE 1.4
TWIN SAMPLE BACKGROUND DATA
INTELLIGENCE

Matrices Grade	I	II	III	IV	V
MZ twins (44 pairs)	32%	40%	23%	2%	3%
DZ twins (51 pairs)	24%	32%	35%	7%	2%

TABLE 1.5
TWIN SAMPLE BACKGROUND DATA
LENGTH OF SEPARATION

	Less than 5 years	More than 5 years
MZ twins (44 pairs)	64%	36%
DZ twins (51 pairs)	61%	39%

the two samples in terms of length of separation, using a cut-off point of 5 years. It can be seen that about 60% of the twins in both groups had been separated for less than that time, this number of course including a very large proportion of pairs who were still living together.

It is clear, then, that while the two types of twin were fairly well matched with respect to the five variables considered, the sample as a whole was not a random one. This fact inevitably limits to some extent the conclusions that can be drawn from the study, though it is worth noting that the particular biases observed in our own group are quite common in twin samples made up of volunteers, as most of them are. A number of twin investigators have reported that it can be difficult finding representative samples, particularly getting older, male, non-identical pairs. In our case the problem was aggravated by the nature of the investigation. Thus, it is easier to obtain more random samples for studies involving the collection of data by postal enquiry. Here, however, we were asking the twins to undertake a sometimes lengthy journey to our laboratory and to take part in an arduous testing programme. On the lighter side, it can be said that for two of the experimenters, at least, the routine of testing was enlivened by having a sample containing so many intelligent, well-bred, dolly girls!

Determination of zygosity

An early criticism of the twin method concerned the unreliability of procedures used to determine the zygosity of twin pairs. If the criticism were ever quite so serious as was once thought it can no longer be said to apply since contemporary techniques make it possible to decide with a high degree of accuracy the probability that a particular pair of twins is genetically identical. The two most precise methods that can be used in adult pairs are skin grafting and blood grouping. For obvious reasons the former is not usually practicable and most investigators rely on evidence obtained from a comparison of twins' blood groups, the mode of inheritance of which is well understood. It should be mentioned that neither method is entirely foolproof for, as Bulmer (op. cit.) discusses, it is possible for blood group chimaerae to be found in human twins. That is to say, because of a fusion of the foetal circulation the blood of a particular pair may consist of a mixture of two distinct types. One consequence of this apparently is that cross-grafting of the skin can be made between the members of such a twin pair. However, Bulmer further points out that blood mixing of this kind must be extremely rare and suggests that in statistical studies of twins the possibility of it being a source of error in zygosity determination can be safely ignored.

Turning to the present study, in the case of those twins who had been subjects of previous investigations and who formed the main nucleus of our sample, the zygosities had already been estimated from blood groups before they came to us. Indeed in a few cases the twins from that sample had volunteered for an investigation of skin grafting being carried out in Glasgow and the results of this procedure were available to us. However, it was considered desirable to start afresh with the zygosity determinations and the University of Glasgow Institute of Genetics was therefore approached for its help. Professor Renwick there advised us that it would be possible to improve on the previous estimations by

TABLE 1.6
MARKERS USED IN DETERMINATION OF TWIN ZYGOSITY

ABO	ABH secretor
MNS	Transferrin
P	Haptoglobin
Rh	Gm and Inv gammaglobulin antigens
Lutheran	Group-specific component
Kell	Serum cholinesterase
Lewis	Phosphoglucomutase$_1$
Duffy	6-phosphogluconate dehydrogenase
Kidd	Adenylate kinase
	Acid phosphatase

adding further markers and he kindly undertook the task of determining the zygosities for us, including those for new twin pairs that were later added to the sample. All twins were referred for zygosity determination unless they showed a gross difference in eye or hair colour, the list of markers used being shown in Table 1.6. Of the markers listed there the red cell antigens were tested by the Department of Haematology at the Southern General Hospital, Glasgow, but the remaining work, including the calculation of the odds on zygosity, was carried out by Professor Renwick and his colleagues.†

The odds on zygosity for each pair tested are shown in Table 1.7, though it should be mentioned that in a few twins, due to technical difficulties, one of the markers was not available. This involved blood grouping systems P (two pairs), MNS (one pair) and ABO (one pair). In these cases the zygosity probabilities were determined on the basis of the remaining markers. It can be seen from Table 1.7 that the range of odds over the group as a whole was from 0·0093 (DZ):1 (MZ) to 0·00076 (DZ):1 (MZ). The highest of these occurred in the case of one of the pairs in whom the P blood group was missing. However, even here the possibility of misclassification was very slight, while the overall error in estimating the zygosities of the twins was satisfyingly small.

Before closing this section brief mention should be made of a "zygosity questionnaire" developed during the course of the twin study. The questionnaire, which is fully described in an appendix to the book, consisted of a short set of items asking the twins about their physical resemblance to each other. It was devised partly as an exercise, in order to decide whether it would be feasible to use the questionnaire method of determining zygosity should we wish, at a future date, to carry out a postal study of twins. Availability of the genetic marker data on all of the twins completing the questionnaire provided us with an ideal opportunity to validate the items. In fact, as the results described in the appendix demonstrate, the questionnaire was highly accurate in discriminating between MZ and DZ twins, despite the fact that, due to an

† The testing of serum and erythrocytic proteins was supported in part by grant G 960/109B from the Medical Research Council to Dr J. H. Renwick. Miss M. M. Izatt, MSc, FIMLT, Dr L. H. Barron, PhD, Miss M. I. Harvie, Mrs J. Black, Mrs M. Campbell and Miss H. Ross are thanked for this part of the work. The calculations of the odds on zygosity were carried out by Dr Renwick and Miss Izatt.

TABLE 1.7

POSTERIOR ODDS ON ZYGOSITY FOR INDIVIDUAL TWIN PAIRS

DZ	:	MZ	DZ	:	MZ
0·00076	:	1	0·0010	:	1
0·0024	:	1	0·00095	:	1
0·0018	:	1	0·0019	:	1
0·0073	:	1	0·0065	:	1
0·0093	:	1	0·0016	:	1
0·0041	:	1	0·0038	:	1
0·0021	:	1	0·0013	:	1
0·0036	:	1	0·0030	:	1
0·0029	:	1	0·0030	:	1
0·0075	:	1	0·0037	:	1
0·0048	:	1	0·0019	:	1
0·0018	:	1	0·0033	:	1
0·00095	:	1	0·0056	:	1
0·0031	:	1	0·0032	:	1
0·0031	:	1	0·0020	:	1
0·0031	:	1	0·0064	:	1
0·0043	:	1	0·0044	:	1
0·0070	:	1	0·0031	:	1
0·0044	:	1	0·0070	:	1
0·0071	:	1	0·0015	:	1
0·0062	:	1	0·0015	:	1
0·0067	:	1	0·0023	:	1

(Each pair listed is classed as monozygotic because the two members of the pair did not differ in any of the polymorphic markers tested, nor in sex. The Bayesian method of Smith and Penrose (1955) was used. A 2:1 weighting in favour of dizygosity was incorporated to allow for its higher frequency. Maternal age, which has an influence on the relative frequency of dizygosity, was not taken into account and the polymorphisms were not scored on other sibs or on the parents.)

oversight, one potentially sensitive item, concerned with eye-colour, was omitted from the questionnaire! The result obtained here is consistent with the findings of other workers who have examined the problem. Thus, Nichols and Bilbro (1966) report accurate diagnosis of zygosity from physical resemblance. The questionnaire and set of rules they developed for doing so were actually much more elaborate than those used here and it is encouraging that even quite crude information about physical similarity allows zygosity to be determined with an acceptably low degree of error. Certainly the error, though not quantifiable, is likely to be so small as to have little material effect on the results of statistical studies of twins using reasonably large samples. This fact would provide some defence, at least, for those earlier twin studies which have been criticized on the grounds that because blood typing methods were not used the zygosity determinations were unreliable.

Despite the convenience of using questionnaires for certain purposes there nevertheless remain two strong arguments in favour of basing determination of zygosity, wherever possible, on genetic polymorphisms; preferably those in which the influence of environmental or chance factors is minimal. First, the genetics of simple polymorphisms can be known by methods not involving twin comparisons; thus avoiding the circularity that is inherent in the use of characteristics, such as eye-colour, where our confidence in the genetic basis itself depends to a large extent on studies of twins. Secondly, within limits, a numerical value can be attached to the zygosity when simple polymorphisms are used. This is particularly important in communicating the confidence of an investigator in his diagnosis of zygosity and was considered a sound reason for adopting the very accurate procedures used in the present study.

Some procedural details

Exact details of the various experimental procedures followed will be described in the particular chapters covering each group of measures. However, some general remarks are necessary about the arrangements that were made for testing the twins and the statistical methods used for analysing the results.

Most of the measurements obtained on the twins, that is those described in Chapters 2, 3 and 4, involved a one-day testing session for each pair who came to the department together. In the morning the battery of personality and cognitive tests was administered to one member of the pair while his or her twin underwent the psychophysiological procedures. During the afternoon session the pair members changed places. In order to control for time of day effects on the psychophysiological measures, the elder and younger twin for consecutive pairs was assigned alternately to these procedures in the morning sessions. At the end of the day both members were taken to the hospital's haematology department so that specimens could be obtained for later zygosity analysis. The twins were then given a small honorarium for taking part in the project.

In the case of the sedation threshold, because of the nature of that procedure, a further visit to the department was necessary. There a number of the twins meeting certain age and health requirements to be described later were asked on their first visit whether they would be willing to volunteer for the test, which was explained fully to them. A mutually convenient time for both members of a pair to come back together was then arranged. Subsequently, as mentioned in the Preface, some of the twins were also asked for their co-operation in various other projects undertaken by ourselves and by other workers given access to our twin register. The results of these studies will be reported elsewhere.

Turning to the statistical methods used here, a number of procedures are available, including several for calculating a so-called "heritability index". These have been concisely summarized by Mittler (op. cit.) whose account will not be replicated here. Suffice it to say that their use seems dubious, since the various procedures often lead to different values of heritability while from a genetic point of view they would appear to be somewhat meaningless. We chose, therefore, to analyse most of our data by calculating two statistics: the intraclass correlation on each measure for MZ and DZ twins and the F-ratio of the MZ and DZ within-pair variances. The latter, expressed as $F = V_{DZ}/V_{MZ}$ would actually seem to be the most informative way of evaluating the intra-pair differences or relative concordances across the two types of twin. The actual similarities found within the MZ and DZ twin samples can then be examined by means of the intraclass correlations, calculated as

$$r_I = \frac{V_b - V_w}{V_b + V_w},$$

where V_b is the variance between and V_w the variance within twin pairs. The significance of the intraclass correlation is tested as the F-ratio of V_b/V_w.

Unless otherwise stated, all of the measurements obtained in the project were analysed according to the above methods.

Concluding remarks

As indicated in this chapter, the project to be described here consisted of a series of studies of different aspects of the behaviour of twins, loosely connected by a nervous typological theory of personality. Thus the orientation of the project was biological in two senses; first, in focusing on the psychophysiological correlates of personality as a source of individual differences and, secondly, in its interest, because of the nature of the people studied, in the genetic basis of behaviour. The studies reported in the following chapters can be perhaps most properly judged, therefore, not solely as experiments in psychogenetics but as investigations in the biological basis of human variation in its widest sense.

References

BROWN, A. M., STAFFORD, R. E. and VANDENBERG, S. G. (1967) Twins: behavioural differences. *Child Develop.* **38**, 1055–64.

BULMER, M. G. (1970) *The Biology of Twinning in Man.* Clarendon Press, Oxford.

CATTELL, R. B. (1965) Methodological and conceptual advances in evaluating hereditary and environmental influences and their interaction. In Vandenberg, S. G. (Ed.) *Methods and Goals in Human Behaviour Genetics.* Academic Press, New York.

CLARIDGE, G. S. (1967) *Personality and Arousal.* Pergamon, Oxford.

CLARIDGE, G. S. (1970) Psychophysiological techniques. In Mittler, P. (Ed.) *The Psychological Assessment of Mental and Physical Handicaps.* Methuen, London.

DARLINGTON, C. D. (1954) Heredity and environment. *Proc. IXth Internat. Congr. Genet. Caryologia* **190**, 370–81.

EYSENCK, H. J. (1960) Levels of personality, constitutional factors, and social influences: an experimental approach. *Int. J. soc. Psychiat.* **6**, 12–24.

EYSENCK, H. J. (1967) *The Biological Basis of Personality.* Charles C. Thomas, Springfield, Ill.

FISHER, R. A. (1918) The correlation between relatives on the supposition of Mendelian inheritance. *Transactions of the Royal Society (Edinburgh)* **52**, 399–433.

GRAY, J. A. (1964) *Pavlov's Typology.* Pergamon, Oxford.

GREENE, W. A. and SWISHER, S. N. (1969) Psychological and somatic variables associated with the development and course of monozygotic twins discordant for schizophrenia. *Ann. N.Y. Acad. Sci.* **164**, 394–408.

JINKS, J. L. and FULKER, D. W. (1970) Comparison of the biometrical genetical, MAVA, and classical approaches to the analysis of human behaviour. *Psychol. Bull.* **73**, 311–49.

JONES, H. E. (1955) Perceived differences among twins. *Eugenics Quart.* **2**, 98–102.

LILIENFELD, A. (1961) Problems and areas in genetic-epidemiologic field studies. *Ann. N.Y. Acad. Sci.* **91**, 797–805.

MATHER, K. (1949) *Biometrical Genetics: the Study of Continuous Variation.* Methuen, London.

MITTLER, P. (1971) *The Study of Twins.* Penguin, London.

MACSWEENEY, D. A. (1970) A report on a pair of male monozygotic twins discordant for schizophrenia. *Brit. J. Psychiat.* **116**, 315–22.

MOSHER, L. R., POLLIN, W. and STABENAU, J. R. (1971) Families with identical twins discordant for schizophrenia: some relationships between identification, thinking styles, psychopathology and dominance-submissiveness. *Brit. J. Psychiat.* **118**, 29–42.

NICHOLS, R. C. and BILBRO, W. C. (1966) The diagnosis of twin zygosity. *Acta Genet. (Basel)* **16**, 265–75.

PILOT, M. L., RUBIN, J., SCHAFER, R. and SPIRO, H. M. (1963) Duodenal ulcer in one of identical twins. *Psychosom. Med.* **25**, 285–91.

SCARR, S. (1968) Environmental bias in twin studies. In Vandenberg, S. G. (Ed.) *Progress in Human Behaviour Genetics.* The Johns Hopkins Press, Baltimore.

SHIELDS, J. (1954) Personality differences and neurotic traits in normal twin school-children. *Eugenics Rev.* **45**, 213–46.

SHIELDS, J. (1962) *Monozygotic Twins Brought Up Apart and Brought Up Together.* Oxford University Press, London.

SMITH, R. T. (1965) A comparison of socioenvironmental factors in monozygotic and dizygotic twins, testing an assumption. In Vandenberg, S. G. (Ed.) *Methods and Goals in Human Behaviour Genetics.* Academic Press, New York.

SMITH, S. M. and PENROSE, L. S. (1955) Monozygotic and dizygotic twin diagnosis. *Ann. hum. Genet.* **19**, 273–89.

CHAPTER 2

PERSONALITY TRAITS IN TWINS

By SANDRA CANTER

Introduction

There has been only a limited number of studies of the hereditary determinants of personality characteristics. Here we are concerned only with those studies using personality questionnaires and there has already been an excellent review of the literature by Vandenberg (1967). Despite the numerous difficulties of such a review, his conclusions were optimistic, suggesting the need for further work in an area where promising results are beginning to emerge. Rather than repeat that review we have reproduced as Table 2.1 Vandenberg's summary of all of those twin studies using questionnaires. Vandenberg's was one of the few attempts to impose a structure on the field by attempting to integrate the findings of studies that had been carried out from several different theoretical viewpoints. His own theory is based largely on that of Heymans, who suggested three major axes of personality which he termed activity, emotionality, and primary versus secondary function. However, a more widely recognized description of personality is that given by Eysenck (1953) whose theory proposes two independent, higher order factors of extraversion–introversion and neuroticism. Indeed, Vandenberg expressed the main conclusions of his review in terms of these more familiar personality variables. He concluded that "we have encountered time and again evidence of a strong hereditary component in sociability or extraversion and its opposite, introversion." The evidence with respect to other major traits, such as neuroticism, he regarded as inconclusive. A similar conclusion was also reached in a more recent review of this field by Mittler (1971).

TABLE 2.1

SUMMARY OF FINDINGS FROM TWIN STUDIES USING PERSONALITY QUESTIONNAIRES
(adapted from Vandenberg, 1967)

Author	Questionnaire	Personality traits		
		MZ significantly more alike than DZ	MZ and DZ equally alike	DZ more alike than MZ
Carter, 1935	Bernreuter	Self-sufficiency Dominance Self-confidence Neuroticism	Introversion Sociability	
Vandenberg, 1962	Thurstone	Active Sociable Vigorous Impulsive	Dominant Stable Reflective	
Cattell et al., 1955 Vandenberg, 1962 Gottesman, 1963a	HSPQ	Neuroticism Surgency Will control Energetic conformity Cyclothymia v. schizothymia	Dominance Cyclothymia Tendermindedness Nervous tension Socialized morale	Impatient dominance

Gottesman, 1963b
Gottesman, 1965
Reznikoff and
  Honeyman, 1967
	MMPI	Social introversion
		Depression
		Psychasthenia
		Psychopathic deviate
		Schizophrenia
		Psychoneurotic
		  complaints
		Psychosomatic
		  complaints
		Masculinity-femininity
			Paranoia
			Hysteria
			Hypochondriasis
			Hypomania
			Masculinity-femininity
			Introversion
			Test-taking attitude	

Wilde, 1964	Amsterdam Biographical Questionnaire	Introversion		
Vandenberg et al., 1966	Myers–Briggs			Thinking-feeling Judgement-perception See-ing-intuiti…

1966	Index factors	Closeness	Motivation / Submissiveness / Friendliness	
Vandenberg et al., 1966	Comrey	Sensuousness, Self-assertion, Applied interests, Orderliness, Expressiveness-constraint, Egoism-diffidence, Educability, Achievement need, Shyness, Compulsion, Religious attitudes	Dependence, Self-control, Empathy, Welfare-state attitude, Punitive attitude, Neuroticism	Hostility, Ascendance
Scarr, 1966	Gough ACL, Fels Behaviour List	Need for affiliation, Friendliness, Social apprehension, Likeableness, Counselling readiness		
Gottesman, 1966	CPI	Dominance, Sociability, Self-acceptance, Originality, Social presence, Good impression, Socialization, Psychological mindedness	Status capacity, Sense of wellbeing, Self-control, Tolerance, Communality, Responsibility, Achievement via independence, Intellectual efficiency, Femininity, Flexibility, Psychoneurotic, Need for achievement, Neuroticism, Aggressiveness, Lack of control	Achievement via conformance
Bruun et al., 1967	Special questionnaire and interview	Sociability, Frequency of drinking, Average consumption		

As can be seen from Table 2.1, these conclusions were based on studies using a variety of tests, many not concerned with major personality factors like extraversion and neuroticism, but with specific traits such as shyness, friendliness and so on. As Vandenberg himself admits, his conclusions are based on the assumption that similar trait names do in fact refer to the same underlying characteristics and that the measures used are reliable and valid. It is perhaps the more surprising, therefore, that some order can be imposed on the results of these studies.

Another point that should be made is that the majority of work has been done with adolescent samples. However, when comparing the results of studies of adolescents with those using adults there are no glaring differences between them, except that changes in the relative importance of hereditary and environmental factors with age would seem to be an important factor requiring investigation.

The present study

The personality measures chosen for study here were mainly, though not entirely, selected on the grounds that they were broadly relevant to the theoretical framework within which the project as a whole had been planned. That is to say, most of the tests were chosen because they were suitable instruments for measuring those descriptive personality characteristics of current interest in nervous typological theory, as outlined in Chapter 1. The actual tests used are listed in Table 2.2.

TABLE 2.2
QUESTIONNAIRES ADMINISTERED AND SAMPLE DETAILS

Questionnaire	Number of twin pairs	
	MZ	DZ
Eysenck Personality Inventory	40	45
Sociability/Impulsivity Scale	40	45
Cattell's 16PF	39	44
Foulds Hostility Scale	39	44

Only one, the Foulds Hostility Scale, had been chosen with no particular personality theory in mind. However, it was of interest for its own sake because it had never previously been included in a twin study. Of the remaining tests the EPI, like its earlier equivalent the MPI, has been extensively used to investigate the biological correlates of extraversion and neuroticism (Eysenck, 1967). The Sociability/Impulsivity Scale was composed of items taken from a paper by Eysenck and Eysenck (1963) on the factorial structure of extraversion. It was of interest because of the possibility that the two components of extraversion may have different descriptive, nervous typological, and genetic characteristics. Finally, the Cattell 16PF was included because, in addition to providing alternative measures of the Eysenck dimensions, its first-order factors allowed a more detailed trait analysis of personality to be carried out.

Of the entire twin sample at our disposal eighty-five pairs completed two or more of the questionnaires, the exact numbers involved in each case being shown, according to zygosity, in Table 2.2. Data were not collected on the remaining available pairs because one or both twins did not complete the questionnaires due to an inability to read, low IQ, or lack of time. Lack of time also accounted for the failure to administer all four questionnaires to all of the twins considered here. Comparison of the MZ and DZ groups shown in Table 2.2 indicated that they did not differ materially from the sample from which they were taken with respect to the matching variables of sex, age, IQ, and social class. However, it will be recalled, as discussed in Chapter 1, that the sample as a whole, and therefore that part of it used here, was not randomly distributed on these variables, but tended to contain a disproportionate number of young, intelligent, middle-class females. This bias should be borne in mind when interpreting the results of the personality data presented below. These will be discussed in two parts. First, the MZ and DZ samples will be compared on each of the personality questionnaires in turn, the groups being considered both as a whole and taking account of sex. Secondly, the samples will be examined in order to determine the influence of age and length of separation on twin similarities and differences.

Comparison of MZ and DZ samples

Eysenck Personality Inventory

The results for this test are given in Table 2.3, where it can be seen that the intraclass correlations for MZ and DZ twins are very similar on

TABLE 2.3
EYSENCK PERSONALITY INVENTORY
INTRACLASS CORRELATIONS AND F-RATIOS: TOTAL GROUP

	r_{MZ}	r_{DZ}	F
Neuroticism	0·37‡	0·23†	1·41
Extraversion	0·34‡	0·29‡	0·99
Number of pairs	40	45	

† $p < 0.05$.
‡ $p < 0.01$.

both extraversion and neuroticism. Furthermore in neither case does the F-ratio indicate a significant difference in the within-pair variances for the two types of twin. Essentially the same results emerged when males and females were considered separately (see Table 2.4). The

TABLE 2.4. EYSENCK PERSONALITY INVENTORY
INTRACLASS CORRELATIONS AND F-RATIOS: SEXES COMPARED

	Females			Males		
	r_{MZ}	r_{DZ}	F	r_{MZ}	r_{DZ}	F
Neuroticism	0·33†	0·20	1·23	0·33	−0·10	2·27
Extraversion	0·29†	0·21	1·06	0·60†	0·59†	0·93
Number of pairs	31	31		9	14	

† $p < 0.05$.
‡ $p < 0.01$.

results therefore provide no evidence for a significant genetic contribution to the two characteristics measured by the EPI.

Judged against Vandenberg's conclusions discussed earlier, the finding here for neuroticism is perhaps not too surprising, since of nine relevant studies quoted by him, four demonstrated no differences between MZ and DZ twins (see Table 2.1). However, the present result is somewhat different from that recently obtained by Young *et al.* (1971) using an updated version of the EPI, the PEN inventory. They concluded that neuroticism was influenced by heredity, though it should be noted that the intraclass correlations for their MZ and DZ samples, while less alike than those reported here, still did not differ significantly.

Young *et al.* also argued that heredity makes a significant contribution to extraversion, again as measured by the PEN questionnaire. The failure here to find such evidence, using an essentially similar scale, is puzzling and, superficially at least, is also at variance with Vandenberg's conclusions. However, his comments were based mainly on studies that were concerned, not with extraversion as a higher order factor, but with specific traits or component parts of it, such as sociability, social introversion, impulsivity and so on. Evidence relevant to this point is described in the next section.

Sociability/Impulsivity Scale

Tables 2.5 and 2.6 give the results obtained here for the two components of extraversion measured by this scale. It can be seen from

TABLE 2.5
SOCIABILITY/IMPULSIVITY SCALE
INTRACLASS CORRELATIONS AND F-RATIOS: TOTAL GROUP

	r_{MZ}	r_{DZ}	F
Sociability	0·67‡	0·25†	2·32‡
Impulsivity	0·24†	−0·03	1·84†
Number of pairs	40	45	

† $p < 0.05$.
‡ $p < 0.01$.

Table 2.5 that in the case of sociability MZ twins as a group were significantly more alike than DZ twins, suggesting that genetic factors make an important contribution to this characteristic. On impulsivity there was a significant difference between the within-pair variances of the two groups but the correlations themselves were low and non-significant.

TABLE 2.6
SOCIABILITY/IMPULSIVITY SCALE
INTRACLASS CORRELATIONS AND F-RATIOS: SEXES COMPARED

	Females			Males		
	r_{MZ}	r_{DZ}	F	r_{MZ}	r_{DZ}	F
Sociability	0·62‡	0·08	2·78‡	0·79‡	0·61‡	1·21
Impulsivity	0·28†	−0·08	2·29†	0·16	0·09	0·99
Number of pairs	31	31		9	14	

† $p < 0.05$.
‡ $p < 0.01$.

Considering the sexes separately (see Table 2.6), it can be seen that the trend found for the group as a whole applied only to females. There was no significant difference between the within-pair variances of the two male samples. This may have been due to the unreliability of the results from such a small sample. Thus, four of the fourteen pairs of DZ twins showed large differences that affected the correlation. However, other studies have found sex differences and therefore these cannot be ruled out (Vandenberg et al., 1966).

It would seem that it is those aspects of extraversion concerned with sociability that are particularly subject to genetic influence, the evidence for impulsivity being less convincing. These findings are consistent with Vandenberg's summary of previous work. He reached his conclusions about the heritability of extraversion mainly on the basis of evidence about sociability, though a few studies were concerned with measuring control of behaviour or its opposite, impulsiveness. Of eight studies concerned with measuring sociability in various forms only one, that by Carter (1933), failed to provide evidence for a significant contribution of genetic factors. Of those studies concerned with measuring some aspect of control of behaviour two have obtained positive results in favour of a genetic hypothesis (Vandenberg, 1962, 1966) and one a negative result (Vandenberg *et al.*, 1966).

16PF Questionnaire

So that a direct comparison can be made with the results of the EPI the second-order factors derived from this test will be discussed first. As can be seen from Table 2.7, while in all cases the correlations for the

TABLE 2.7
16PF SECOND-ORDER FACTORS
INTRACLASS CORRELATIONS AND F-RATIOS: TOTAL GROUP

	r_{MZ}	r_{DZ}	F
Neuroticism	0·36†	0·06	1·30
Anxiety	0·56‡	0·33‡	1·34
Extraversion	0·43‡	0·08	1·36
Number of pairs	39	44	

† $p < 0.05$.
‡ $p < 0.01$.

DZ twins were lower than those for MZ twins, there were no significant differences between the within-pair variances for the two samples. This confirms the results for the EPI, the general trend being in the direction of greater similarity among MZ twins but the differences not reaching significance. When taking males and females separately (see Table 2.8) the results for the females were similar to those for the total sample. In the case of males the MZ/DZ differences were even less marked, the correlations for the Anxiety factor actually being reversed, with DZ twins being more alike than MZ twins.

TABLE 2.8

16PF SECOND-ORDER FACTORS

INTRACLASS CORRELATIONS AND F-RATIOS: SEXES COMPARED

	Females			Males		
	r_{MZ}	r_{DZ}	F	r_{MZ}	r_{DZ}	F
Neuroticism	0·35‡	−0·02	1·20	0·32	0·18	1·80
Anxiety	0·49‡	−0·13	1·38	0·01	0·38	1·29
Extraversion	0·54‡	0·20	1·51	0·66†	0·52†	1·04
Number of pairs	30	30		9	14	

† $p < 0.05$.
‡ $p < 0.01$.

The results for the first-order factors are presented in Table 2.9. Four of the factors showed a significant difference between MZ and DZ twins. These were factors B (Intelligence), I (Tough versus Tender-mindedness), L (Trusting versus Suspicious), and O (Placid versus Apprehensive). As with the second-order factors the results proved to be different for males and females taken separately (see Table 2.9). For the female sample significant differences were found between the two types of twin on Factors I and L only and, for the males, on factors O and B only. The implication of these results is difficult to decide upon because of the small number of male pairs involved.

To facilitate interpretation of the first-order factor data, those factors (I, L and O) showing a significant MZ/DZ difference were correlated with the three 16PF second-order factors and with the two scales from the EPI. These results are shown in Table 2.10. It can be seen that correlations, where they existed, were with anxiety/neuroticism and not at all with extraversion. This was particularly so of L and O, perhaps not unexpectedly since they are component parts of the 16PF Anxiety factor. It would seem, then, that as in the case of extraversion it is only certain traits making up anxiety/neuroticism, rather than the general dimension itself, which has a significant genetic loading.

TABLE 2.9
16PF First-order factors
Intraclass correlations and F-ratios

	Total group			Females			Males		
	r_{MZ}	r_{DZ}	F	r_{MZ}	r_{DZ}	F	r_{MZ}	r_{DZ}	F
A (Reserve)	0·49‡	0·21†	1·02	0·53‡	0·33‡	0·80	0·37	0	1·10
B (Intelligence)	0·23†	0·13	1·84†	0·17	0·35‡	1·34	0·43	−0·40	4·10†
C (Stability)	0·37‡	0·15	1·03	0·35‡	0·12	1·00	0·47	0·25	1·27
E (Assertiveness)	0·27†	0·30‡	1·10	0·17	0·09	1·00	0·67†	0·56†	2·19
F (Sobriety)	0·56‡	0·47‡	0·98	0·54‡	0·26†	1·23	0·67†	0·81‡	0·44
G (Expedience)	0·14	0·34‡	0·77	0·19	0·17	0·85	−0·06	0·61‡	0·66
H (Shyness)	0·58‡	0·30‡	1·48	0·55‡	0·27†	1·33	0·73‡	0·29	2·20
I (Tough-mindedness)	0·68‡	0·25†	2·89‡	0·64‡	0·25†	3·09‡	0·69†	0·22	2·53
L (Trust)	0·34‡	0·05	1·74†	0·46‡	−0·18	2·25†	−0·42†	0·49	0·82
M (Imaginativeness)	0·23†	0·08	1·47	0·23	0·11	1·62	0·24	−0·04	1·11
N (Shrewdness)	0·19	0·30‡	0·84	0·17	0·24	0·81	−0·08	0·38	1·18
O (Placidness)	0·38‡	0·06	1·89†	0·34‡	0·06	1·37	0·79‡	0·05	15·54‡
Q1 (Conservativeness)	0·25†	0·09	0·89	0·16	0·09	0·89	0·55†	0·13	0·98
Q2 (Group-dependence)	0·39‡	0·01	1·26	0·42‡	−0·07	1·51	0·38	0·25	0·76
Q3 (Self-conflict)	0·22†	0·23†	0·80	0·43‡	0·17	1·25	−0·31†	0·34	0·32
Q4 (Tension)	0·20	0·10	0·77	0·27†	0·01	0·70	−0·25†	0·26	0·99
Number of pairs	39	44		30	30		9	14	

† $p < 0.05$.
‡ $p < 0.01$.

TABLE 2.10

CORRELATIONS OF THE SIGNIFICANT FIRST-ORDER FACTORS WITH THE
SECOND-ORDER FACTORS OF THE 16PF AND WITH THE EPI

	16PF Second-order factors			EPI scales	
	N	A	E	N	E
16PF First-order factors					
I (Tough-minded vs. tender-minded)	0·25†	−0·06	0·10	0	−0·08
L (Trusting vs. suspicious)	0·35†	0·56‡	0	0·36‡	−0·02
O (Placid vs. apprehensive)	0·76‡	0·76‡	−0·21†	0·57‡	−0·12

† $p < 0.05$.
‡ $p < 0.01$.

Foulds Hostility Scale

As can be seen in Table 2.11, there was a significant difference between the two types of twin on the measures of self-criticism and intropunitiveness. As with the other questionnaires there were some differences between male and female twins, though in this case they were relatively slight. The Foulds scale has not previously been used in a study of this kind, few workers having tried to measure such traits in twins. However, Vandenberg *et al.* (1966), using the Comrey personality and attitude scales, did find a significant difference between female MZ and DZ twins on a measure of punitiveness. Results for a hostility measure were negative in both males and females.

The study just described and the findings reported here would support the view that at least certain features of hostility may be partly determined by genetic factors. On the other hand, it is possible that the findings simply represent the contribution of heredity to more stable personality dimensions associated with hostility, such as extraversion and neuroticism. This interpretation would be supported by the cor-

TABLE 2.11
FOULDS HOSTILITY SCALE
INTRACLASS CORRELATIONS AND F-RATIOS

	Total group			Females			Males		
	r_{MZ}	r_{DZ}	F	r_{MZ}	r_{DZ}	F	r_{MZ}	r_{DZ}	F
Acting out hostility	0·14	0·30‡	0·75	0·21	0·44‡	0·69	−0·12	−0·04	0·77
Criticism of others	0·38‡	0·09	1·36	0·40‡	0·13	0·98	0·21	0·02	2·40
Delusional hostility	0·26†	0·01	0·51	0·13	0·05	0·39	0·49	−0·05	0·70
Self-criticism	0·56‡	−0·04	2·68‡	0·52‡	−0·18†	2·68‡	0·60†	−0·03	3·26
Delusional guilt	0·07	0·08	0·78	0·05	0·11	0·75	0·25	0·38	1·55
Extrapunitiveness	0·41‡	0·22†	1·19	0·39‡	0·32†	0·88	0·41	0·06	1·94
Intropunitiveness	0·43‡	−0·02	2·20‡	0·38‡	−0·14	2·00	0·57†	−0·01	3·39†
General hostility	0·39‡	0·04	1·52	0·48‡	0·07	1·80	0·28	0·04	1·04
Direction of hostility	0·41‡	0·23†	1·08	0·24†	0·10	0·93	0·73‡	0·01	2·24
Number of pairs	39	44		30	30		9	14	

† $p < 0.05$.
‡ $p < 0.01$.

relations observed here between the other personality measures used and the two scales of hostility showing MZ/DZ differences, viz. self-criticism and intropunitiveness. The correlations between these various measures are shown in Table 2.12. It can be seen that both hostility

TABLE 2.12

CORRELATIONS OF THE SIGNIFICANT SCALES OF THE FOULDS HOSTILITY SCALE WITH THE 16PF SECOND-ORDER FACTORS AND WITH THE EPI

Hostility Scale	EPI		16PF		
	N	E	N	A	E
Self-criticism	0·60‡	−0·27‡	0·57‡	0·61‡	−0·40‡
Intropunitiveness	0·62‡	−0·21‡	0·60‡	0·63‡	−0·33‡

† $p < 0.05$.
‡ $p < 0.01$.

scales correlated significantly and positively with the several measures of anxiety/neuroticism. They also correlated negatively and significantly, if to a slightly lesser extent, with the various measures of extraversion and its component parts. The MZ/DZ twin differences observed on the Foulds scale were therefore probably due to associated variations in anxiety/neuroticism and extraversion. In so far as the latter dimensions can be said to be subject to genetic influence, to that extent hereditary factors would appear to contribute to the way in which the individual expresses hostility.

The influence of age and separation

It is important to know whether personality differences are stable over time, mainly because one would expect a trait which is to a great extent genetically determined to be relatively invariant compared with one that is largely environmental in origin. This is not to say that we cannot expect any fluctuation since all personality traits, however large the genetic component, will be subject to environmental modification.

A powerful factor influencing personality at the descriptive level will be human interaction. In this respect, of course, twins are in a unique position and we might expect that the twin situation itself will affect the expression of certain personality characteristics. The twin situation is not only of interest in its own right but also because it has implications for the way we interpret the statistical comparisons on which herit- ability estimates are based. Thus, the correlation observed between members of a twin pair will reflect both their common genetic back- ground and their shared environments, including their interaction with each other. As discussed in the previous chapter, the end-result may be one of exaggerating or it may be one of minimizing the phenotypic similarity of twins.

The most elegant way to examine the influence of the twin situation on behavioural traits is to study pairs that have been separated from birth. This, of course, could not be done within the design of the present investigation. However, it was possible to look at the effects of *relative* separation on twin similarity by making comparisons between pairs according to the length of time they had been living apart, either because of marriage or occupation. For the present purposes a suitable cut-off point was considered to be five years. The twins were therefore divided into two groups: those who, when first seen by us, had been living apart for more than five years and those who had been separated for a shorter time than that, the latter actually consisting mainly of pairs who were still living together. For convenience these groups will sometimes be referred to below as the "separated" and "unseparated" twins respectively. Within each of the groups the MZ and DZ samples were compared on all of the personality tests described previously.

Table 2.13 gives the results of this comparison for extraversion and neuroticism as measured by the EPI and for the three second-order factors of the 16PF. It can be seen that on Anxiety and on both measures of neuroticism twin pairs, whether MZ or DZ, were more alike when together or recently separated than when they had been separated for more than five years. The exception was for MZ twins on the 16PF Neuroticism factor, where separation appeared to have no effect. A comparison of MZ and DZ twins by means of the F-ratio revealed that there was no significant difference between the two types in the effect of separation on anxiety/neuroticism. These results of course confirm

TABLE 2.13

INTRACLASS CORRELATIONS AND F-RATIOS FOR "SEPARATED" AND "UNSEPARATED" TWINS EPI AND 16PF SECOND-ORDER FACTORS

	r_{MZ}		r_{DZ}		F-ratio	
	Less than 5 yrs	More than 5 yrs	Less than 5 yrs	More than 5 yrs	Less than 5 yrs	More than 5 yrs
EPI { Neuroticism	0·53‡	0·18	0·70‡	−0·17	0·94	1·76
Extraversion	0·10	0·67‡	0·22	0·36	0·68	2·11
Number of pairs	25	15	29	16		
16PF { Neuroticism	0·37†	0·37	0·32†	−0·26	0·95	1·77
Anxiety	0·56‡	0·27	0·44‡	−0·53‡	1·70	1·55
Extraversion	0·29	0·85‡	−0·65‡	0·50‡	3·60†	2·29
Number of pairs	23	15	28	16		

† $p < 0.05$.
‡ $p < 0.01$.

the earlier finding for the samples as a whole in suggesting that hereditary factors contribute very little to anxiety/neuroticism measured as a higher order dimension of personality. On the contrary, breakdown of the groups in terms of separation suggests that there are powerful influences operating within the twin situation which determine whether the members of a pair report themselves as being equally neurotic or not. This seemed to be particularly true of DZ pairs where there were quite marked differences in the intraclass correlations for "unseparated" and "separated" twins; for example, a change from significantly positive ($+0.44$) to significantly negative (-0.53) on the 16PF Anxiety factor.

Turning now to extraversion, it can be seen from Table 2.13 that the pattern of correlations was quite the reverse of that just described for anxiety/neuroticism. That is to say, both types of twin were more alike in extraversion when apart than when together. This is particularly true of MZ twins where for both the EPI and 16PF measures the correlations were low and non-significant in "unseparated" pairs but highly significantly positive in "separated" pairs. For DZ twins, results were less consistent across the two personality tests. On the EPI measure of extraversion little effect of separation was apparent, but on the 16PF the correlation was significantly negative in "unseparated" and significantly positive in "separated" twins.

It can be seen in Table 2.13 that of the F-ratio comparisons between the MZ and DZ groups one was significant. Moreover, the relative sizes of the correlations in the separated MZ and DZ samples were in favour of a genetic explanation of extraversion. The correlations were respectively $+0.67$ and $+0.36$ for the EPI and $+0.85$ and $+0.50$ for the 16PF. Taken altogether these results might help to explain why, when separation was not taken account of and the sample was considered as a whole, no evidence was found for a genetic contribution to extraversion on the two tests. Thus the results suggest that the effect of the interaction between members of a twin pair in close contact with each other is to make them less alike in extraversion, perhaps because they tend to adopt complementary roles. It is only after separation, when the modifying influences arising from the twin situation are eliminated or reduced, that the genotypic similarities can be fully expressed at the phenotypic level.

The samples of twins used in the above comparisons were small and the evidence therefore only suggestive. However, changes in the correlations between twins with separation were also obtained in a study by Wilde (1964). He also took five years as a cut-off point and obtained the results shown in Table 2.14. Of the variables of interest the most

TABLE 2.14
INTRACLASS CORRELATIONS FOR MZ AND DZ TWINS LIVING TOGETHER (T) OR
APART (A) ON THREE PERSONALITY SCALES (TAKEN FROM WILDE, 1964)

	MZ		DZ	
	T	A	T	A
Psychoneurotic complaints	0·55	0·52	−0·14	0·28
Psychosomatic complaints	0·46	0·75	−0·05	0·64
Extraversion	0·58	0·19	0·19	0·36
Number of pairs	50	38	21	21

striking results were those for psychosomatic complaints, those twins living apart being more alike than those living together. This was particularly true of the DZ twins, though the difference between DZ and MZ twins was significant only for those twins who were together; suggesting a possible hereditary factor that expresses itself later when the twins become separated. In so far as psychosomatic complaints can be said to be associated with anxiety/neuroticism, Wilde's results are opposite to those reported here, though clearly the two sets of data are not entirely comparable.

On his measure of extraversion Wilde also found somewhat different results. As shown in Table 2.14 his MZ twins who were living together were *more* alike than those living apart. However, the reverse was true for DZ twins who behaved more like the present DZ sample. Clearly the effects of separation on extraversion are not entirely consistent from one study to the next, but the findings are of general interest in emphasizing how twin pairs can become more or less similar according to the closeness of contact between them.

TABLE 2.15

INTRACLASS CORRELATIONS AND F-RATIOS FOR "SEPARATED" AND "UNSEPARATED" TWINS
SOCIABILITY/IMPULSIVITY SCALE

	r_{MZ}		r_{DZ}		F-ratio	
	Less than 5 yrs	More than 5 yrs	Less than 5 yrs	More than 5 yrs	Less than 5 yrs	More than 5 yrs
Sociability	0·51‡	0·91‡	0·25	0·25	1·41	9·50‡
Impulsivity	−0·03	0·20	−0·26	0·35	2·12	0·91
Number of pairs	25	15	29	16		

† $p < 0.05$.
‡ $p < 0.01$.

Returning to the present data, the results of analysing the effects of separation on the two components of extraversion, sociability and impulsivity, are shown in Table 2.15. With the exception of sociability in "separated" DZ twins, the effects of separation on both components were similar to those found for extraversion measured as a composite dimension. That is to say, "separated" twins were more alike than those who were not separated. However, in the case of impulsivity the correlations were very low and, as before, it was sociability that showed the most clear-cut evidence of genetic determination. Thus, in MZ twins the correlation for this component rose from $+0.51$ in "unseparated" to $+0.91$ in "separated" pairs. In DZ pairs the comparable values both remained at $+0.25$. The F-ratio for the difference in within-pair variances was very highly significant. These results therefore confirm that it is sociability that is mainly responsible for the observed genetic determination of extraversion and that, like the latter, close contact between members of an MZ twin pair tends to hide genotypic similarities that only find phenotypic expression after the twins are separated for a relatively long period of time.

Examination of the 16PF first-order factors from a similar point of view revealed a complex pattern of results, presented in Table 2.16. The four factors B, I, L and O found to differentiate MZ and DZ twins in the total group will be discussed first. On the Intelligence factor (B) separation had no effect in MZ twins, but tended to make DZ twins less similar. On the other three factors separation either had no effect or tended to reduce the intraclass correlations for MZ and DZ pairs alike. The most marked difference occurred on factor O (Placid versus Apprehensive) where the correlation for MZ twins dropped from $+0.50$ in "unseparated" to $+0.27$ in "separated" pairs. F-ratio comparisons on these four factors indicated that where there were significant differences in the MZ and DZ within-pair variances they always involved twins separated for less than five years. These results therefore resemble those reported earlier for the second-order Anxiety and Neuroticism factors, namely a tendency for separation to reduce twin similarity. They are also consistent with the correlations shown to exist between anxiety/neuroticism and factors I, L and O (see Table 2.10).

Of the remaining 16PF first-order factors, M (Practical versus Imaginative) showed some differences between MZ and DZ pairs, but

TABLE 2.16

INTRACLASS CORRELATIONS AND F-RATIOS FOR "SEPARATED" AND "UNSEPARATED" TWINS 16PF FIRST-ORDER FACTORS

	r_{MZ}		r_{DZ}		F-ratio	
	Less than 5 yrs	More than 5 yrs	Less than 5 yrs	More than 5 yrs	Less than 5 yrs	More than 5 yrs
A (Reserve)	0·38†	0·62‡	0·25	0·02	0·87	1·49
B (Intelligence)	0·20	0·16	0·26	−0·29	1·81	1·91
C (Stability)	0·50‡	0·22	0·22	−0·03	1·23	0·88
E (Assertiveness)	0·13	0·37	0·18	0·37	1·10	1·12
F (Sobriety)	0·42†	0·79‡	0·24	0·60‡	0·83	1·49
G (Expedience)	0·30	−0·02	0·23	0·51†	1·24	0·37
H (Shyness)	0·57‡	0·63‡	0·28	0·35	1·44	1·52
I (Tough-mindedness)	0·67‡	0·70‡	0·20	0·36	3·25†	2·34
L (Trust)	0·38†	0·24	0·07	0·01	1·96	1·58
M (Imaginativeness)	0·32	0·17	0·19	−0·16	1·97	1·17
N (Shrewdness)	0·34†	0·03	0·41†	0·07	0·87	0·86
O (Placidness)	0·50‡	0·27	0·18	−0·19	2·22†	1·71
Q1 (Conservativeness)	0·16	0·42	0·28	−0·09	0·51	1·82
Q2 (Group-dependence)	0·32	0·49†	−0·10	0·37	1·61	0·51
Q3 (Self-conflict)	0·33	0·11	0·22	0·07	0·98	0·66
Q4 (Tension)	0·49‡	−0·11	0·23	−0·06	1·15	0·62
Number of pairs	23	15	28	16		

† $p < 0.05$.
‡ $p < 0.01$.

TABLE 2.17

INTRACLASS CORRELATIONS AND F-RATIOS FOR "SEPARATED" AND "UNSEPARATED" TWINS
FOULDS HOSTILITY SCALE

	r_{MZ}		r_{DZ}		F-ratio	
	Less than 5 yrs	More than 5 yrs	Less than 5 yrs	More than 5 yrs	Less than 5 yrs	More than 5 yrs
Acting out hostility	0·09	0·19	0·44‡	0·06	0·61	1·03
Criticism of others	0·41†	0·31	0·19	−0·09	1·32	1·44
Delusional hostility	0·48‡	0·13	0·14	−0·06	0·60	0·52
Self-criticism	0·62‡	0·50†	0·11	−0·29	3·20†	2·61†
Delusional guilt	0·23	−0·10	0·15	0·08	1·81	0·71
Extrapunitiveness	0·41†	0·39	0·34†	0·04	1·21	1·31
Intropunitiveness	0·56‡	0·28	0·22	−0·23	2·45†	2·07
General hostility	0·56‡	0·24	0·22	−0·17	2·14†	2·06
Direction of hostility	0·33	0·49†	0·30	0·12	1·26	0·88
Number of pairs	23	15	28	16		

† $p < 0.05$.
‡ $p < 0.01$.

the actual correlations were low and the result difficult to interpret. Several of the other factors also showed some separation effect. Factor F (Sober versus Happy-go-lucky) showed a tendency for separation to increase similarity regardless of zygosity, while the opposite was true of factors N (Forthright versus Shrewd) and Q4 (Relaxed versus Tense). On one factor, G (Expedient versus Conscientious) separation had different effects in the two types of twin, MZ pairs becoming less and DZ pairs more alike.

Finally, for the Foulds Hostility Scale there was little evidence of a marked separation effect on the two characteristics shown earlier to differentiate MZ and DZ twins (see Table 2.17). The DZ pairs did become somewhat less alike in self-criticism when separated, but the previously observed significant difference between MZ and DZ twins on this trait remained regardless of separation. A somewhat similar result emerged for intropunitiveness, except that the F-ratio was significant only for the comparison between "unseparated" pairs.

It is clear that one factor complicating the interpretation of all of the results reported so far in this section is that of age, since using the criterion of separation adopted here, those twins classified as living apart for more than five years inevitably tended to be older. In order to assess the additional influence of age on twin similarities and differences a further analysis of the data was undertaken, this time comparing twins who were less than with those who were more than twenty-one years old at the time of testing. The results of this analysis are shown in Tables 2.18 to 2.21.

The findings can be very briefly summarized. The effects of age were almost identical to those of separation in the case of the EPI scales and the 16PF second-order factors (Table 2.18) and in the case of the Sociability/Impulsivity measures (Table 2.19). That is to say, increasing age tended to make twins less alike in anxiety/neuroticism but more alike in extraversion, particularly sociability. Age and separation also had broadly similar effects on the 16PF first-order factors (Table 2.20) and Foulds Hostility Scale scores (Table 2.21). Although inspection of the tables will reveal some minor differences these are impossible to interpret and, for want of a better explanation, might be put down to experimental error.

Because the separation and age factors examined here are so closely

TABLE 2.18

INTRACLASS CORRELATIONS AND F-RATIOS FOR YOUNGER AND OLDER TWINS
EPI AND 16PF SECOND-ORDER FACTORS

	r_{MZ}		r_{DZ}		F-ratio	
	Less than 21 yrs	More than 21 yrs	Less than 21 yrs	More than 21 yrs	Less than 21 yrs	More than 21 yrs
EPI { Neuroticism	0·63‡	0·20	0·56‡	−0·02	1·29	1·67
Extraversion	0·14	0·50‡	0·22	0·36	0·85	1·18
Number of pairs	20	20	26	19		
16PF { Neuroticism	0·49‡	0·28	0·28	−0·06	1·05	1·65
Anxiety	0·70‡	0·21	0·20	−0·02	1·73	1·41
Extraversion	0·17	0·80‡	−0·78‡	0·59‡	3·84‡	1·36
Number of pairs	20	19	26	18		

† $p < 0.05$.
‡ $p < 0.01$.

TABLE 2.19

INTRACLASS CORRELATIONS AND F-RATIOS FOR YOUNGER AND OLDER TWINS
SOCIABILITY/IMPULSIVITY SCALE

	r_{MZ}		r_{DZ}		F-ratio	
	Less than 21 yrs	More than 21 yrs	Less than 21 yrs	More than 21 yrs	Less than 21 yrs	More than 21 yrs
Sociability	0·49†	0·85‡	0·21	0·47†	1·40	5·37‡
Impulsivity	−0·09	0·21	−0·26	0·22	1·86	1·09
Number of pairs	20	20	26	19		

† $p < 0.05$.
‡ $p < 0.01$.

TABLE 2.20

INTRACLASS CORRELATIONS AND F-RATIOS FOR YOUNGER AND OLDER TWINS
16PF FIRST-ORDER FACTORS

	r_{MZ}		r_{DZ}		F-ratios	
	Less than 21 yrs	More than 21 yrs	Less than 21 yrs	More than 21 yrs	Less than 21 yrs	More than 21 yrs
A (Reserve)	0·43	0·58‡	0·21	0·12	0·98	1·08
B (Intelligence)	0·24	0·11	0·22	−0·08	1·96	1·64
C (Stability)	0·46	0·32	0·35†	−0·03	0·81	1·32
E (Assertiveness)	0·21	0·31	0·08	0·46†	1·44	0·86
F (Sobriety)	0·41	0·76‡	0·19	0·68‡	0·84	1·15
G (Expedience)	0·15	0·12	0·14	0·43†	1·03	0·60
H (Shyness)	0·49	0·65‡	0·12	0·45†	1·48	1·40
I (Tough-mindedness)	0·69	0·67‡	0·22	0·33	3·15†	2·53†
L (Trust)	0·40	0·29	−0·16	0·11	1·76	1·81
M (Imaginativeness)	0·16	0·27	0·25	−0·18	1·98	1·30
N (Shrewdness)	0·21	0·20	0·43†	0·08	0·75	0·98
O (Placidness)	0·67	0·19	0·29	−0·09	2·10	2·08
Q1 (Conservativeness)	0·23	0·30	0·29	−0·08	0·52	1·52
Q2 (Group-dependence)	0·33	0·40†	−0·10	0·27	1·85	0·51
Q3 (Self-conflict)	0·25	0·20	0·19	0·13	0·81	0·83
Q4 (Tension)	0·55	−0·08	0·13	0·06	1·15	0·68
Number of pairs	20	19	26	18		

† $p < 0.05$.
‡ $p < 0.01$.

TABLE 2.21
INTRACLASS CORRELATIONS AND F-RATIOS FOR YOUNGER AND OLDER TWINS
FOULDS HOSTILITY SCALE

	r_{MZ}		r_{DZ}		F-ratio	
	Less than 21 yrs	More than 21 yrs	Less than 21 yrs	More than 21 yrs	Less than 21 yrs	More than 21 yrs
Acting out hostility	−0·08	0·27	0·40†	0·13	0·60	0·97
Criticism of others	0·48	0·30	−0·04	0·22	1·62	1·16
Delusional hostility	0·49	0·12	0·14	−0·05	0·52	0·55
Self-criticism	0·65	0·49†	−0·05	−0·04	3·24†	2·61†
Delusional guilt	0·37	−0·18	0·10	0·18	2·34†	0·61
Extrapunitiveness	0·48	0·36	0·20	0·21	1·32	1·22
Intropunitiveness	0·64	0·21	0·08	−0·01	2·90†	1·90
General hostility	0·58	0·27	0	0·05	2·06	2·12
Direction of hostility	0·48	0·38†	0·25	0·23	1·62	0·76
Number of pairs	20	19	26	18		

† $p < 0.05$.
‡ $p < 0.01$.

correlated, it is clearly difficult to disentangle their relative contributions to twin similarities and differences. However, it is perhaps reasonable to argue that age, if it has an effect on personality traits, tends to produce differentiation and should therefore bring about dissimilarity rather than similarity between members of twin pairs. If that is true the results found here for extraversion, and its component sociability, would seem unlikely to be due to the age variable. It is more probable, as suggested earlier, that they were a consequence of the twin situation, the degree of phenotypic similarity varying inversely with the extent of interaction between pair members. A similar argument cannot, however, be advanced in the case of anxiety/neuroticism and its component parts, since the diminished similarity observed with separation could have been due to the age factor. Had the sample been larger it would have been possible to determine the relative importance of these two variables by looking at the influence of one while holding the other constant. However, in the absence of appropriate data the problem must remain for further research.

Discussion and conclusions

The results reported in this chapter are clearly very complex and do not permit any simple statement about the contribution of heredity to personality as measured in terms of descriptive traits and dimensions of behaviour. Such a conclusion is not surprising; indeed it was anticipated, for the purpose of the study was not to arrive at heritability estimates but rather to explore the problem of genetic/environmental interaction in the personality sphere, trying to identify processes or aspects of personality that might deserve further examination from a similar point of view. Having done so, several conclusions can be reached.

One is that, contrary to some opinion, it would seem more profitable to examine the genetic basis of personality, not in terms of very general dimensions, like extraversion, but in terms of more specific components of these broad factors. Of the major personality dimensions studied here, extraversion would certainly seem to have important genetic determinants, though this is largely a reflection of the strong influence of heredity on one of its components, namely sociability. With regard to anxiety/neuroticism, there seems to be no evidence for any marked contribution of heredity although there was a suggestion here that some traits associated with it might be partly under genetic control.

A second conclusion to be reached from the present study is that factors operating within the twin situation itself may have very powerful effects on the personality similarities and differences observed in twin pairs. These effects will depend on the particular characteristic involved and upon the nature of the twins' relationship, as reflected in their age and degree of separation. Close contact between the members of a twin pair, particularly at an early age, would, according to the evidence obtained here, tend to make them less like each other in sociability but to have more neurotic traits in common. Later separation and/or age reverse both of these trends so that the twin interaction appears to have the overall effect of masking quite striking genetic influences on sociability and of capitalizing on a relatively weak contribution of heredity to anxiety/neuroticism. Methodologically these age and separation effects are important because they illustrate the dangers of uncritically interpreting intraclass correlations as evidence for or against genetic explanations of behaviour. Thus correlations obtained on young twins still living together might lead the investigator to reach quite different conclusions from those measured on older pairs, the members of which were having relatively little influence on each other's behaviour. Depending on the characteristic studied, the role of heredity in determining individual differences might be overestimated or underestimated. In general, as far as personality traits are concerned, it would seem most logical to seek heritability estimates in those twins who are currently living apart, rather than together. In that way the "suppressor" effects of the twin situation such as occurred here in the case of sociability would be minimized. At the same time exaggerated estimates of heritability would be avoided in the case of those traits which twins share because of mutual interaction. Of course, the problem is methodologically important only if the effects described depend on zygosity or, put more precisely, if the interaction between MZ pairs is more powerful than that between DZ pairs. Some of the results reported here suggest that this might be the case, the correlations in MZ and DZ pairs sometimes becoming more markedly different in older separated twins.

Methodology aside, the twin situation and the interaction between members of a twin pair is a topic of great interest in its own right. It is, however, one which has been relatively neglected in a field where the study of twins is most often undertaken with the aim of being able to make statistical statements about the fractions of behaviour that can be assigned to genetic factors. We have deliberately avoided trying to do so here and, while the investigation of the twin situation was not our main purpose, some of the relationships between genetic and environmental factors in personality suggested by the present study do seem sufficiently important to warrant further research.

References

BRUUN, K., MARKKANEN, T. and PARTENEN, J. (1967) *Inheritance of Drinking Behaviour, a Study of Adult Twins*. Finnish Foundation for Alcohol Studies, Helsinki.

CARTER, H. D. (1933) Twin similarities in personality traits. *J. genet. Psychol.* **43**, 312–21.

CARTER, H. D. (1935) Twin similarities in emotional traits. *Character and Personality* **4**, 61–78.

CATTELL, R. B., BLEWETT, D. B. and BELOFF, J. R. (1955) The inheritance of personality: multiple-variance analysis of approximate nature–nurture ratios for primary personality factors in Q-data. *Amer. J. hum. Genet.* **7**, 122–46.

EYSENCK, H. J. (1953) *The Structure of Human Personality*. Methuen, London.

EYSENCK, H. J. (1967) *The Biological Basis of Personality*. Charles C. Thomas, Springfield, Ill.

EYSENCK, H. J. and EYSENCK, S. B. G. (1963) On the dual nature of extraversion. *Brit. J. soc. clin. Psychol.* **2**, 46–55.

GOTTESMAN, I. I. (1963a) Genetic aspects of intelligent behaviour. In Ellis, N. (Ed.) *Handbook of Mental Deficiency: Psychological Theory and Research*. McGraw-Hill, New York.

GOTTESMAN, I. I. (1963b) Heritability of personality: a demonstration. *Psychol. Monogr.* **77**, 9, whole number 572.

GOTTESMAN, I. I. (1965) Personality and natural selection. In Vandenberg, S.G. (Ed.) *Methods and Goals in Human Behaviour Genetics*. Academic Press, New York.

GOTTESMAN, I. I. (1966) Genetic variance in adaptive personality traits. Paper presented to the American Psychological Association.

MITTLER, P. (1971) *The Study of Twins*. Penguin Books, London.

REZNIKOFF, M. and HONEYMAN, M. S. (1967) MMPI profiles of monozygotic and dizygotic twin pairs. *J. consult. Psychol.* **31**, 100.

SCARR, S. W. (1966) The origins of individual differences in adjective check list scores. *J. consult. Psychol.* **30**, 354–7.

VANDENBERG, S. G. (1962) The hereditary abilities study: hereditary components in a psychological test battery. *Amer. J. hum. Genet.* **14**, 220–37.

VANDENBERG, S. G. (1966) The contributions of twin research to psychology. *Psychol. Bull.* **66**, 327–52.

VANDENBERG, S. G. (1967) Hereditary factors in normal personality traits (as measured by inventories). In Wortis, J. (Ed.) *Recent Advances in Biological Psychiatry*, vol. 9, pp. 65–104. Plenum Press, New York.

VANDENBERG, S. G., STAFFORD, R. E., BROWN, A. and GRESHAM, J. (1966) *The Louisville Twin Study*. University of Louisville School of Medicine, Louisville, Kentucky.

WILDE, G. J. S. (1964) Inheritance of personality traits. *Acta Psychologica* 22, 37–51.

YOUNG, J. P. R., FENTON, G. W. and LADER, M. H. (1971) The inheritance of neurotic traits: a twin study of the Middlesex Hospital Questionnaire. *Brit. J. Psychiat.* 119, 393–8.

CHAPTER 3

SOME ASPECTS OF COGNITIVE FUNCTION IN TWINS

By SANDRA CANTER

Introduction

There is considerable evidence for the importance of genetic factors in the determination of general intelligence (Burt, 1966; Erlenmeyer-Kimling and Jarvik, 1963). However, Vandenberg (1966) suggested that, while one would always expect to find a factor of general intelligence in a battery of cognitive tests, there is also sufficient evidence for a number of separate abilities and that it would therefore seem appropriate to study hereditary factors in each of these abilities individually. He reviewed a number of studies which had found significant differences between MZ and DZ twins on several factors from the test of primary mental abilities (Blewett, 1954; Thurstone *et al.*, 1955; Vandenberg, 1962, 1965). Vandenberg attempted to assess whether such differences as were observed for the separate abilities were related, in the sense that general intelligence could be said to account for all of the hereditary variance. He used a multivariate analysis of covariance of twin differences on the data of his own 1962 study and obtained four significant roots of the six primary mental abilities. He concluded that these were four independent hereditary components, a suggestion which confirms that it may be fruitful to investigate a range of cognitive factors rather than make general comparisons on measures of global intelligence.

In his excellent discussion of intelligence Butcher (1970) included a large number of areas of investigation of what could loosely be called cognitive processes. His view exemplifies the much broader approach taken in recent years towards the concept of intelligence. He included in his account of the topic both work from experimental psychology, mainly concerned with concept attainment and brain and machines, as well as attempts that have been made to measure the creative process. Two of the cognitive processes from these wider areas of study were the focus of the present research. It was decided to investigate two aspects of cognitive functioning that have been given little attention in the field of psychogenetics, namely *divergent thinking* and *conceptual ability*. There were a number of reasons for selecting these two areas, besides the interest of the author and the obvious lack of knowledge about hereditary factors involved in them.

With regard to divergent thinking there has been considerable controversy in recent years as to its relationship with general intelligence, as measured by standard tests. The impetus for the discussion came from the statement by Getzels and Jackson (1962) that there is no relationship between intelligence and creative thinking. Their work has received criticism from several investigators (Burt, 1962; De Mille and Merrifield, 1962). More recent studies on unselected populations of school children have found substantial correlations between intelligence and creativity (Edwards and Tyler, 1965; Hasan and Butcher, 1966). To account for these discrepancies it has been suggested that there is a relationship between IQ and creativity up to a level of about 120 points but that above this level creativity is not necessarily associated with intelligence (Yamamoto, 1964; More, 1966). It has also been suggested that factors such as school atmosphere and methods of teaching (Torrance, 1965), as well as conditions of test administration (Wallach and Kogan, 1965), are responsible for the findings. Wallach and Kogan found that when tests were administered in a relaxed atmosphere and were untimed, relationships between creativity tests were themselves lower than those between creativity and intelligence.

Since it has become widely accepted that general intelligence as measured by standard tests is in part due to heredity, it was thought of interest to investigate whether there was any evidence that genetic factors also play a part in creative ability, at least as measured in a very limited sense by divergent thinking tests. If such tests are closely correlated with intelligence test measures one would expect to find similar differences between MZ and DZ twins as those observed for general intelligence.

The problem of cognitive function was also approached in the present study with an interest in abnormal processes and their manifestation in a normal population. Hence our second special area of investigation, that of conceptual thinking. Many investigators have studied the abnormal conceptual thinking of psychiatric patients, particularly in schizophrenics. This abnormal thinking has been variously described, but here we were concerned with what has been termed overinclusive thinking, a characteristic of some schizophrenic patients. This has been defined as a broadening of conceptual span to the inclusion of irrelevant thoughts and ideas and has been measured by a variety of conceptual sorting tests. It has been suggested that thinking of an overinclusive type is not restricted to schizophrenic patients, but can be found in a normal population (McConaghy and Clancy, 1968). It has also been shown that parents of schizophrenic patients with thought disorder of this type also show overinclusive thinking more frequently than a random group of normals (McConaghy, 1959; Phillips et al., 1965). Furthermore, McConaghy and Clancy (1968) recently found that where normal subjects do show overinclusion their parents also tend to, though to a lesser degree than in the case of schizophrenics' parents. These results have been quoted as supporting a genetic explanation of overinclusive thinking. Accepting that there are many difficulties inherent in its measurement (Hawks, 1964; Price, 1970), nevertheless it was considered useful to include in the present study a comparison of MZ and DZ twins on a number of tests purporting to measure overinclusion.

Choice of the two areas of cognitive function just described was not, of course, coincidental, since there are theoretical reasons for believing that divergent thinking and overinclusion may represent different aspects of the same underlying process. One line of argument leading to this view is derived from work in normal psychology on "cognitive control principles" or "cognitive styles" (Gardner et al., 1959; Klein, 1958). These response dispositions are said to determine an individual's perception and conceptual thinking and to be related to certain personality characteristics (Witkin et al., 1962; Silverman, 1964; Klein, op. cit.). One cognitive control principle is concerned with the extent to which the individual scans his environment (Gardner, 1961) and Silverman (op. cit.) has suggested that scanning may be involved in creative thinking as well as being responsible for certain forms of psychotic thinking.

In abnormal psychology itself it has also been argued that over-inclusive thinking and unusual types of thought arise from a disorder of attention in which there is an inability to inhibit irrelevant stimuli (Payne, 1960; Claridge, 1967); a form of response not dissimilar to scanning as described by cognitive control theorists. More broadly, a comparison has often been made between psychotic and creative thinking, a similarity commented upon many years ago by Kretschmer (1931) and discussed more recently by McConaghy (1960, 1961) and by Claridge (1972).

The hypothesis that there may be similarities between the processes involved in both creative thinking and schizophrenic thinking, due to a similarity in attention or cognitive style, would therefore appear to be worth investigating. Here we are concerned only in a limited way with such an hypothesis. No attempt was made to measure either creativity, as such, or psychosis; but only to investigate the relationship between a number of tests of divergent thinking and several conceptual measures that have been used to study overinclusion or abnormal conceptual thinking in schizophrenic patients.

There have been only very few attempts previously to look at such relationships but the results have been encouraging. Spotts and Mackler (1967) found a positive correlation between field independence and creativity, while Baggerley (1955) reported a relationship between conceptual thinking and style of performance on a number of other cognitive tests. In an interesting extension of their study of creativity Wallach and Kogan (op. cit.) found a tendency for creativity as measured by psychometric tests to be associated with an unconventional and free type of response on the Goldstein Scheerer object sorting test. This kind of response is also common in some types of schizophrenic patient given the latter test (Payne and Hewlett, 1960).

Divergent thinking

The term creative thinking has been used a number of times throughout the previous discussion, but it would be unwise to conclude that we have as yet developed any "true" measures of this ability. However, there is a range of tests which, it is claimed, measure some aspects of the creative process. Of these the most comprehensive and widely used are those of Guilford and Torrance. Their tests attempt to measure such processes as flexibility, elaboration, and originality of thinking. They have been severely criticized on the grounds that there is insufficient evidence about their reliability and validity. There are in fact few studies of the tests from that point of view and those that exist have depended on external criteria which in themselves are of doubtful value. Indeed, the problem that besets this field is one of finding suitable external criteria. Usually school grades, nominations, and performance records of various kinds have been used, but there have been few long-term follow-up studies to demonstrate their predictive value. The tests themselves are also cumbersome to score and objectivity is difficult to maintain without losing valuable qualitative aspects of performance. Because of the many disadvantages of such tests it might be considered premature to use them in a study such as this. However, as no alternatives were available it was decided to proceed, using some of the Guilford measures.

Guilford (1967) has constructed a highly detailed classification of human abilities. One process involved he has termed divergent thinking defined as the "generation of information from given information, where emphasis is upon variety and quantity of output from the same source likely to involve transfer". It is contrasted with convergent thinking which involves achieving one correct, conventional solution to a given problem. As a result of a number of factor analytic studies Guilford has emerged with a number of factors important in divergent thinking, such as fluency, flexibility, originality, analysis and synthesis, and evaluation. A large number of tests have been proposed to measure these factors, the test content being of a semantic, figural, or symbolic type. For the purpose of the present study five tests only were chosen in an attempt to measure the three factors of fluency, flexibility and originality and to cover both semantic and figural content. Fluency has been divided into ideational, associational, and expressional forms, but all essentially concern the ease with which ideas are generated. Flexibility has been divided up into spontaneous and adaptive types, the former being the ability to change from one idea to another and the latter the ability to use ideas from a known situation in a new and unknown one. Originality is the ability to produce new and uncommon responses.

Description of tests

Word Association. This test consisted of a list of twenty-five words with multiple meanings. Subjects were instructed to write down as many meanings as they could for each word. They were told that they would obtain a score both for the number of words given and for the number of different meanings offered. Fifteen minutes were allowed for completion. Two scores were obtained, as follows:

1. The total number of responses given, providing a measure of ideational fluency.
2. The total number of different types of response given, providing a measure of semantic flexibility.

Unusual Uses. Here subjects were given the names of five objects: a brick, a paper clip, a toothpick, a pencil, and a sheet of paper. They were asked to write down as many different uses for each object as they could. Fifteen minutes were allowed for completion. Three scores were obtained, as follows:

1. The total number of responses given, providing a measure of ideational fluency.
2. The number of different types of use given, providing a measure of semantic flexibility.
3. The uniqueness of the responses given, providing a measure of originality.

The last of these scores was determined by calculating the frequency of each response across the sample. This distribution was then divided into fifths, a score of five being given for the least frequent responses through four, three, and two, down to one for the most frequent.

Consequences. This test consisted of four statements suggesting the possibility of certain eventualities, subjects being required to state what they thought would happen if the changes described in the statements occurred. For example, they were asked what would happen if all national and local laws were abolished. The total time allowed for the test was fifteen minutes, subjects being required to write down as many different answers to each statement as they could.

As used by Guilford, this test yields, in addition to total response score, two other measures, one of direct and the other of indirect, or original, consequences. An attempt was made here to use a similar scoring procedure by getting independent raters to assess the originality of all of the responses given to the test. However, inter-rater reliabilities proved to be so low that a different scoring system, allowing more objectivity, was adopted. The frequency with which each type of response occurred across the sample was first calculated and cast into a distribution. The latter proved to be clearly bimodal, dividing into those responses given by many subjects and those given by only one or two. Responses occurring only once or twice were therefore regarded as original and assigned a score of "one", others being scored zero. For each subject, then, two scores were obtained from the test, as follows:

1. The total number of responses given, providing a measure of fluency.
2. A score of originality, calculated as just described.

Gottschaldt Figures. This was a modification of the hidden figures test developed originally by Gottschaldt (1926). It had previously been used by Guilford (1967) as a measure of adaptive flexibility and consisted of four sets of figures, each having a simple geometrical shape hidden in a more complex contour. Subjects were required to find the hidden shape in each figure, the score obtained from the test being the total number of shapes correctly identified.

Making Objects Test. Here subjects were given five sets of different shapes, i.e. of triangles, circles, squares and rectangles, and were instructed to combine them in as many ways as possible to form objects which they were asked to name. The subjects were told that they could use as many, or as few, shapes as they wished in making a particular object and were given fifteen minutes to complete the test. Five scores were obtained, as follows:

1. The total number of shapes used, as a measure of fluency.

2. The total number of different *types* of shape used, as a measure of flexibility.
3. The total number of objects drawn, as a measure of fluency.
4. The total number of different *types* of object drawn, as a measure of flexibility.
5. The quality of drawings, as a measure of originality.

This last score was based on the frequency with which each type of drawing appeared in the whole group, a score of "one" being assigned to those that were found only once. The present criterion of originality was adopted because it was considered to be more objective than that used by Guilford, who relied on judges' assessment of the frequency and combinations of shapes selected and the complexity and interest of the figures produced.

Analysis of divergent thinking measures

As mentioned earlier, Guilford found fluency, flexibility and originality to be three independent factors and in designing the present study the original plan was to use the various scores described in the previous section as measures of these three factors. However, before proceeding to the comparison of MZ and DZ twins it was considered necessary to examine the factorial structure of the test battery in order to determine the validity of the different measures. All of the scores obtained from the five tests were therefore intercorrelated and a principal components analysis, with Varimax rotation, performed on the data. The results of this analysis are shown in Table 3.1, which incidentally also contains the loadings for the Mill Hill Vocabulary Scale, Progressive Matrices, and age. However, as these variables will be discussed more fully later, they will be ignored for the present.

Inspection of Table 3.1 reveals that there is no evidence for the three factors described by Guilford. The five factors obtained, in fact, correspond closely to the five tests entered into the analysis; that is, with the possible exception of Factor 1. The latter is highly loaded on the Word Association test, intelligence, and to a lesser extent on the Gottschaldt Figures and Consequences tests. However, it does not appear to be clearly related to either flexibility, fluency, or originality as such. Factor 2 could be clearly identified with the Objects test, Factor 3 with the

TABLE 3.1

PRINCIPAL COMPONENTS ANALYSES OF DIVERGENT THINKING MEASURES

ROTATED FACTOR LOADINGS

Test	Score	Factor				
		1	2	3	4	5
Word Association	Fluency	−0·79	−0·24	0·36	−0·03	−0·07
	Flexibility	−0·80	−0·25	0·38	−0·02	−0·09
Unusual Uses	Fluency	−0·27	−0·33	0·81	−0·14	0·01
	Flexibility	−0·31	−0·29	0·87	−0·13	0
	Originality	−0·27	−0·26	0·91	−0·09	−0·04
Consequences	Fluency	−0·49	−0·32	0·27	−0·60	0·01
	Originality	−0·34	−0·29	0·21	−0·60	0·07
Making Objects	Fluency (Shapes)	−0·31	−0·62	0·17	−0·17	0·05
	Flexibility (Shapes)	−0·24	−0·88	0·18	−0·15	0
	Fluency (Drawings)	−0·14	−0·93	0·21	−0·08	−0·04
	Flexibility (Drawings)	−0·11	−0·92	0·21	−0·05	−0·05
	Originality	−0·03	−0·63	0·24	0	−0·32
Gottschaldt Figures	Flexibility	−0·51	−0·14	0·04	−0·01	−0·68
Age		−0·18	0	0·02	0·79	0·16
Progressive Matrices		−0·74	−0·13	0·10	0·07	−0·21
Mill Hill Vocabulary		−0·65	−0·01	0·28	−0·36	−0·14

N = 170 subjects.

Uses test, Factor 4 with the Consequences test, and Factor 5 with the Gottschaldt Figures.

There was, therefore, no support for the existence of the three factors which the various tests had purported to measure; nor did the pattern of factor loadings suggest any rationale for dividing the tests on the basis of their verbal or figural content—another "dimension" of divergent thinking it had been hoped to investigate. In view of this finding it was decided to simplify the scoring system used so as to obtain one score for each of the tests from which more than one measure had originally been obtained; that is, all but the Gottschaldt Figures, the score for which remained as before. For the other four tests the following scores were calculated:

Word Association. The total number of responses given.
Unusual Uses. A combination of total number of responses, number of different types of response, and uniqueness score.

TABLE 3.2
DIVERGENT THINKING TESTS
CORRELATIONS BETWEEN TOTAL SCORE MEASURES

	Word Association	Unusual Uses	Consequences	Making Objects	Gottschaldt Figures	Total
Word Association	—	0·60‡	0·51‡	0·44‡	0·45‡	0·72‡
Unusual Uses		—	0·51‡	0·49‡	0·28‡	0·88‡
Consequences			—	0·48‡	0·30‡	0·45‡
Making Objects				—	0·31‡	0·45‡
Gottschaldt Figures					—	0·77‡
Total						—

† $p < 0.05$. In all cases $N = 170$.
‡ $p < 0.01$.

Consequences. A combination of total number of responses and originality score.

Making Objects. A combination of the total number of shapes, the total number of different types of shape, and the originality score.

The intercorrelations between these scores and the Gottschaldt Figures score are shown in Table 3.2. It was considered that these correlations were high enough to justify adding the measures from the five tests together to obtain a total divergent thinking score; thus giving six scores on which the twin analysis could be carried out.

Comparison of MZ and DZ twins

Table 3.3 presents the intraclass correlations and F-ratios of the within-pair variances for the MZ and DZ twins over the sample as a whole and for males and females separately. Taking the group as a whole, though four out of five correlations for the individual tests were higher in MZ than in DZ twins, the only significant F-ratio was for Word Association. The correlations for the two groups on this measure were, however, very similar. This was due to the fact that the between-pair variance of the DZ twins was much greater than that of the MZ twins. The F-ratio of course only takes into account the within-pair variance and as such is a more accurate reflection of the differences between the two types of twin. There is some evidence therefore that on this test MZ twins are more alike than DZ twins.

In the case of female pairs the correlation for the DZ twins was higher than for the MZ twins on the association test, but the significant F-ratio reflects a bigger within-pair variance in the former than in the latter. Again the between-pair variance for DZ twins was twice that of MZ twins, thus giving a misleading intraclass correlation. Clearly where there are such obvious differences in the distribution of scores, results such as those just described have to be interpreted with caution.

There was also a significant difference between MZ and DZ female twins on the Consequences test. The results for the male twins were different in that there was only a significant difference between the two types of twin on the Gottschaldt Figures. As this group was so small no emphasis will be placed on these results. However, the findings for the female sample would suggest the importance of looking at sex

TABLE 3.3
DIVERGENT THINKING TESTS
INTRACLASS CORRELATIONS AND F-RATIO COMPARISONS OF MZ AND DZ TWINS

	Total group		
	r_{MZ}	r_{DZ}	F-ratio
Word Association	0·49‡	0·44‡	1·70†
Unusual Uses	0·52‡	0·34‡	1·12
Consequences	0·52‡	0·22†	1·18
Making Objects	0·21†	0·28‡	0·75
Gottschaldt Figures	0·43‡	0·29†	1·36
Total	0·43‡	0·50‡	1·01
Number of pairs	40	45	

	Male twins			Female twins		
	r_{MZ}	r_{DZ}	F-ratio	r_{MZ}	r_{DZ}	F-ratio
Word Association	0·60†	0·25	1·20	0·43‡	0·49‡	1·94†
Unusual Uses	0·69†	0·09	2·48	0·46‡	0·47‡	0·80
Consequences	0·38	0·37	0·26	0·67‡	0·18	3·16†
Making Objects	0·35	0·26	0·62	0·14	0·30†	0·80
Gottschaldt Figures	0·62†	−0·05	3·28†	0·40‡	0·37‡	0·98
Total	0·53†	0·17	0·93	0·37‡	0·59‡	1·02
Number of pairs	9	14		31	31	

† $p < 0.05$.
‡ $p < 0.01$.

differences, since there significant results were obtained that were not apparent in the group as a whole.

If we interpret the significant F-ratio found in the total group as suggesting the importance of hereditary factors in determining performance on the associations test, it is interesting that this was the test that was highly loaded on Factor 1 in the principal components analysis described earlier and that Factor 1 was also loaded highly on intelligence. In other words, the MZ/DZ differences on the associations test may simply reflect a genetic contribution to intelligence.

The general relationship between creativity and intelligence has already been referred to earlier and was examined further here by looking at the correlations between Progressive Matrices and Mill Hill Vocabulary performance and the single score for each divergent thinking test used in the twin analysis.† These correlations, which are shown in Table 3.4, were all significant and were of the same order as those of the divergent thinking tests with each other (see Table 3.2).

Although these results confirm that divergent thinking and general intelligence are closely related abilities, further analysis of the data suggested that the association between the two was not uniform at all IQ levels. This was shown by dividing the group of subjects into those above and those below the 90th percentile, doing this for both intelligence tests in turn. Correlations between divergent thinking and intelligence were then calculated separately in the two groups. The results of this analysis are shown in Table 3.5, where it can be seen that in subjects falling above the 90th percentile on the Progressive Matrices there was a tendency for the correlations between intelligence and divergent thinking test performance to drop considerably. In fact, many of the correlations for this group were negative. However, with the exception of the Gottschaldt Figures, this trend was not evident in the case of the Mill Hill Vocabulary test.

These findings would suggest that high scoring on those tests used

---

† While some investigators have preferred to enter only one member of each twin pair into correlations, here we have utilized the total sample of subjects so that in all cases the N's are twice the number of available pairs, MZ and DZ combined. That virtually identical results are obtained whichever convention is followed is illustrated for the data in Table 3.4 which, for comparative purposes, shows correlations calculated according to both methods.

TABLE 3.4

CORRELATIONS OF DIVERGENT THINKING TESTS WITH INTELLIGENCE

	Progressive Matrices r	Mill Hill r
Word Association	0·53‡ (0·56‡)	0·55‡ (0·47‡)
Unusual Uses	0·34‡ (0·38‡)	0·46‡ (0·40‡)
Consequences	0·37‡ (0·39‡)	0·45‡ (0·41‡)
Making Objects	0·31‡ (0·38‡)	0·29‡ (0·27‡)
Gottschaldt Figures	0·46‡ (0·47‡)	0·39‡ (0·37‡)
Total	0·47‡ (0·48‡)	0·52 (0·50‡)
N	170	170

† $p < 0·05$.
‡ $p < 0·01$.

Note: Values in brackets are correlations calculated on samples of 85
subjects, i.e. where only one member of each pair of twins has
been entered into the computation (see text).

here, except Gottschaldt Figures, depends on verbal intelligence at all
levels but that above the 90th percentile performance IQ is not important. It is also interesting to note that there was a tendency for
correlations between the divergent thinking tests themselves to decline
at higher IQ levels, indicating that once intelligence becomes less
important in performance the tests are measuring different abilities from
each other.

With regard to intelligence itself, it can be seen from Table 3.6 that
there was a significant difference between MZ and DZ twins on both the
Progressive Matrices and the Mill Hill Vocabulary Scale. As this
supports previous findings, confirming the importance of genetic
factors in intelligence, it would be expected that the difference between
MZ and DZ twins on divergent thinking tests would be related to the
association between those tests and intelligence. That this is so is
demonstrated in Fig. 3.1. There the correlation of each divergent

TABLE 3.5
CORRELATIONS OF DIVERGENT THINKING TESTS WITH INTELLIGENCE
COMPARISON IN HIGH AND LOW INTELLIGENCE

	Progressive Matrices	
	Below 90th Percentile r	Above 90th Percentile r
Word Association	0·44‡	−0·05
Unusual Uses	0·24†	−0·27†
Consequences	0·31‡	0·16
Making Objects	0·22†	−0·01
Gottschaldt Figures	0·37‡	0·04
Total	0·36‡	−0·10
N	104	66

	Mill Hill	
	Below 90th Percentile r	Above 90th Percentile r
Word Association	0·45‡	0·44‡
Unusual Uses	0·32‡	0·36†
Consequences	0·37‡	0·23
Making Objects	0·16	0·13
Gottschaldt Figures	0·33‡	0·12
Total	0·36	0·35†
N	129	41

† $p < 0.05$.
‡ $p < 0.01$.

TABLE 3.6

INTELLIGENCE TESTS

INTRACLASS CORRELATIONS AND F-RATIO COMPARISONS OF MZ AND DZ TWINS

	r_{MZ}	r_{DZ}	F-ratio
Progressive Matrices	0·68‡	0·46‡	3·04‡
Mill Hill Vocabulary	0·85‡	0·68‡	2·02†

† $p < 0·05$.
‡ $p < 0·01$.

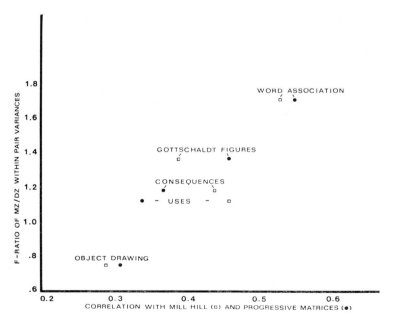

FIG. 3.1. Diagram showing the orderly relationship between the degree to which each divergent thinking test differentiates MZ and DZ twins, as measured by the F-ratios for within-pair variances, and the correlations of those tests with intelligence, as measured by the Mill Hill Vocabulary Scale and the Progressive Matrices.

thinking test with intelligence is plotted against the F-ratio of the MZ/ DZ comparison for the test. It can be seen that for the Progressive Matrices the greater the correlation between intelligence and divergent thinking the greater the difference between MZ and DZ twins. This was slightly less true for the Mill Hill, but the overall tendency is the same. In other words it would seem that general intelligence accounts for a great deal of the hereditary variance on the divergent thinking tests, presumably this being especially so at lower IQ levels.

Finally, it was decided to investigate the stability of the MZ/DZ differences in divergent thinking by examining the influence of age and separation. As for the personality data the separation effect was looked at by comparing twins who had been living apart for more than or less than five years. It can be seen from Table 3.7 that in twins who had been separated for less than that time the F-ratios between MZ and DZ pairs were significant both for the Word Association and Consequences tests. None of MZ/DZ differences was significant for twins separated for more than five years. That this may have been due, in part, to age can be seen from Table 3.8, since the same results were obtained when the sample was subdivided into younger and older twins, using a cut-off point, as before, of twenty-one years. It would appear, therefore, that hereditary factors are important on these two tests only in twin pairs who are younger or who are still living together. It is also worth noting that this trend was also found for general intelligence.

Summary and discussion

To summarize the results of this part of the study, it was found for the total group of twins that there was a significant difference between MZ and DZ pairs on only one divergent thinking test, namely Word Association. However, there was a definite tendency for the differences between the two types of twin to increase as the correlation between the divergent thinking tests and intelligence rose. The association test was the most highly related to intelligence and it was considered that the latter may account for much of the hereditary variance on divergent thinking measures in general. Analysis of the effect of age and years of separation on twin similarity suggested that the extent to which twins resemble each other in divergent thinking is influenced by both of these variables.

TABLE 3.7

DIVERGENT THINKING TESTS

INTRACLASS CORRELATIONS AND F-RATIOS IN "SEPARATED" AND "UNSEPARATED" TWINS

	r_{MZ}		r_{DZ}		F-ratio	
	Less than 5 yrs	More than 5 yrs	Less than 5 yrs	More than 5 yrs	Less than 5 yrs	More than 5 yrs
Word Association	0·49‡	0·51†	0·46‡	0·43†	2·43†	1·15
Unusual Uses	0·52‡	0·53†	0·49‡	0·05	0·81	1·82
Consequences	0·74‡	0·07	0·22	0·16	2·62†	0·41
Making Objects	0·21	0·24	0·36†	0·09	0·76	0·75
Gottschaldt Figures	0·68‡	−0·01	0·43‡	−0·01	1·87	1·10
Total	0·38†	0·53†	0·62‡	0·16	0·78	1·55
Progressive Matrices	0·65‡	0·38	0·65‡	0·06	3·14†	3·18†
Mill Hill	0·88‡	0·74‡	0·75‡	0·48†	1·76	2·34†
Number of pairs	25	15	29	16		

† $p < 0.05$.
‡ $p < 0.01$.

TABLE 3.8

DIVERGENT THINKING TESTS

INTRACLASS CORRELATIONS AND F-RATIOS IN YOUNGER AND OLDER TWINS

	r_{MZ}		r_{DZ}		F-ratio	
	Less than 21 yrs	More than 21 yrs	Less than 21 yrs	More than 21 yrs	Less than 21 yrs	More than 21 yrs
Word Association	0·60‡	0·44†	0·42†	0·47†	2·79†	1·20
Unusual Uses	0·59‡	0·43†	0·45‡	0·13	0·91	1·41
Consequences	0·75‡	0·09	0·15	0·27	2·85†	0·41
Making Objects	0·33	0·13	0·36†	0·13	0·87	0·68
Gottschaldt Figures	0·65‡	0·18	0·48‡	0·10	1·29	1·52
Total	0·47†	0·41†	0·60‡	0·24	0·87	1·21
Progressive Matrices	0·75‡	0·34	0·58‡	0·34	4·71†	2·68†
Mill Hill	0·89‡	0·73‡	0·75‡	0·50†	1·98	2·18†
Number of pairs	20	20	26	19		

† $p < 0.05$.
‡ $p < 0.01$.

It is difficult to evaluate all of the results described here since there have been few previous studies of divergent thinking from a genetic viewpoint; though a number of investigators using the Primary Mental Abilities test have obtained evidence for an hereditary component in the word fluency score (Thurstone *et al.*, 1955; Blewett, 1954; Vandenberg, 1962, 1965). While the relationship between the word fluency factor and the Word Association test used here is unknown it would seem likely that there are similarities between them. On the other hand, Vandenberg (1967) failed to find any difference between MZ and DZ twins on one of Guilford's word association tests. His study is the only one that used a large number of Guilford's divergent thinking tests. On nine such tests, including "pertinent questions", "figure production", "association", and "picture arrangement", only the first yielded a significant MZ/DZ difference. A number of studies have included a version of the Gottschaldt Figures or "concealed figures test" (Vandenberg, 1962; Thurstone *et al.*, 1955; Stuart *et al.*, 1965). The results have suggested the importance of genetic factors here, though in the present study an MZ/DZ difference in Gottschaldt Figures performance was less evident, being shown only by male twins.

Conceptual thinking

As mentioned earlier, the second area of cognitive functioning we were interested in, namely conceptual thinking, has been studied especially in relation to the abnormalities of thought process found in schizophrenia. In that context conceptual thinking has been commonly investigated using sorting tests of various kinds, in which the subject is required to arrange, classify, or select stimulus material according to a number of concepts (Goldstein, 1939; Payne and Hewlett, 1960; Chapman and Taylor, 1957). The performance of schizophrenics on such tests is said to show a number of characteristics, but has frequently been studied under the heading of "overinclusion", the loosening of conceptual boundaries described earlier. Since it was this aspect of conceptual thinking, and to some extent its opposite "overexclusion", with which we were concerned here, a number of appropriate tests were selected for investigation.

Description of tests

Payne Object Classification Test (POCT). This test consists of four triangles, four circles, and four squares varying in size, thickness, colour, material, and area. The subject is required to sort the objects into groups in as many ways as possible, each time following one simple principle. There are ten correct sorting methods, termed A responses, all other methods being called Non-A responses and being regarded by Payne (1962) as indicative of overinclusion. Here both the A response and Non-A response scores were recorded.

Chapman Card Sorting Test 1 (CT1). This test was originally designed by Chapman (1956) to measure the effect of distraction on the conceptual performance of schizophrenics. As used here the material consisted of seventy-two sets of cards presented one at a time to the subject. Each set was made up of three stimulus cards arranged in a row before the subject and one response card placed below it. In the corners of all of the cards was drawn a common object belonging to one of a number of conceptual categories like "figures", "sports equipment", "furniture", "transport" and so on. The task was to match one of the objects on the response card with an object in the bottom right-hand corner of one of the stimulus cards. In each case there was only one correct response, all other objects being irrelevant and acting as distractors. According to the way different sets of cards were arranged, correct matchings could be made on the basis of either identical or conceptual relations between the two objects. That is, the correct object on the response card could either be *identical to* or *of the same type as* the one with which it was matched on the stimulus cards. For example, in the latter case a "shoe" and a "coat" may be matched together.

The following scores were obtained from this test:

1. *Identity error* (S)—error when correct matching was of identical objects.
2. *Conceptual error* (R)—error when correct matching was of conceptually related objects.
3. *Distractor error* (D)—incorrect placement of the response card with a stimulus card containing the distractor figure.

4. *Irrelevant error* (I)—incorrect placement of the response card with a stimulus card containing unrelated objects.
5. *Total error* (T).

Chapman Card Sorting Test 2 (*CT*2). This test was originally devised by Chapman (1961) to measure both overinclusive and overexclusive thinking in schizophrenics. As used here it consisted of twelve sets of ten cards, each containing the name of an object, animal, or plant. Subjects were required to sort the cards into groups according to the particular concept given to them in the instructions. The number of cards given to the subject varied from thirty to sixty, and the instructions referred either to a narrow or to a broad concept. It was expected that when a narrow concept was given there would be more errors of an overinclusive type and that when a broad concept was given there would be more errors of an overexclusive type. Although a large number of scores could be derived from the original test, only the following two were used here:

1. *Total overinclusive errors* (OIT).
2. *Total overexclusive errors* (OET).

Comparison of MZ and DZ twins

The results on the three tests are given in Table 3.9, for the total group, and in Table 3.10 for the male and female twins separately. There was no evidence for an hereditary component in performance on the Payne Object Classification Test, though the correlation for the MZ twins was much larger than for DZ twins on the Non-A score. This was due to the large between-pair variance in the former group and in terms of intra-pair difference scores the DZ twins were, in fact, more alike. There was, however, a significant difference between the two types of twin on the Chapman Test 1 and on the overinclusive score of Chapman Test 2. In the second case the correlations themselves were extremely low and very similar, owing to the large between-pair variance of the DZ group. The results of the CT1, however, do suggest that hereditary factors may be important in conceptual performance where the ability to exclude irrelevant stimuli is involved. These findings also held for the female, but not for the male, half of the sample. In males,

TABLE 3.9

CONCEPTUAL TESTS

INTRACLASS CORRELATIONS AND F-RATIOS: TOTAL GROUP

Test	Score	r_{MZ}	r_{DZ}	F-ratio
Payne OCT	A-responses	0·41‡	0·57‡	0·79
	Non-A responses	0·48‡	0·12	0·38
Chapman Test 1	S errors	0·39‡	0·11	1·24
	R errors	0·28†	0·15	1·90†
	D errors	0·29†	0·06	1·81†
	I errors	0·34†	0·31†	2·10†
	Total errors	0·42‡	0·14	1·81†
Chapman Test 2	Overinclusive errors	0·16	0·12	1·96†
	Overexclusive errors	0·50‡	0·43‡	1·63
Number of pairs		40	45	

† $p < 0.05$.
‡ $p < 0.01$.

because of the peculiarly large variances sometimes found, many of the correlations for MZ pairs were negative, some being higher in the DZ group.

As seen in Table 3.11, all of the tests described in this section were significantly related to intelligence. However, it is interesting that the two scores most highly correlated with intelligence, the A response score on the POCT and the overexclusive score on the CT2, did not show a significant difference between the MZ and DZ twins. This is particularly surprising in the case of the former which is a measure of conceptual ability. It is possible therefore that the differences between MZ and DZ twins, and hence the evidence for genetic determination, found on the Chapman tests were not due to the latters' correlation with general intelligence, but reflected a genuine influence of heredity on overinclusion as a distinct feature of cognitive functioning.

Relationships between divergent and conceptual thinking

As discussed at the beginning of this chapter, the two areas of cognitive function studied here were chosen because it was considered that

TABLE 3.10
CONCEPTUAL TESTS
INTRACLASS CORRELATIONS AND F-RATIOS: SEXES COMPARED

Test	Score	Males			Females		
		r_{MZ}	r_{DZ}	F	r_{MZ}	r_{DZ}	F
Payne OCT	A-responses	0·52	0·43†	1·25	0·39†	0·62‡	0·67
	Non-A responses	0·86‡	0·60‡	0·26	0·04	0·07	0·43
Chapman Test 1	S errors	−0·06	0·03	0·52	0·46‡	0·11	1·57
	R errors	−0·18	0·31	0·69	0·47†	0·09	3·20‡
	D errors	0·10	0·06	1·19	0·37†	0·06	2·13†
	I errors	−0·34	0·74‡	0·50	0·50†	0·11	3·39‡
	Total errors	−0·08	0·27	0·65	0·56†	0·10	2·73‡
Chapman Test 2	Overinclusive errors	0·15	0·06	1·45	0·14	0·20	2·14†
	Overexclusive errors	0·83‡	0·21	2·21	0·38†	0·44‡	1·65
Number of pairs		9	14		31	31	

† $p < 0.05$.
‡ $p < 0.01$.

TABLE 3.11
CORRELATIONS OF CONCEPTUAL TESTS WITH INTELLIGENCE

Test	Score	Progressive Matrices r	Mill Hill Vocabulary r
Payne OCT	A responses	0·48‡	0·43‡
	Non-A responses	0·20‡	0·17†
Chapman Test 1	S errors	−0·44‡	−0·39‡
	R errors	−0·40‡	−0·38‡
	D errors	−0·31‡	−0·22‡
	I errors	−0·43‡	−0·44‡
	Total errors	−0·45‡	−0·42‡
Chapman Test 2	Overinclusive errors	−0·24‡	−0·21‡
	Overexclusive errors	−0·52‡	−0·51‡

† $p < 0.05$.   In all cases $N = 170$.
‡ $p < 0.01$.

there may be a theoretical link between them, in so far as divergent thinking and overinclusion may refer to different aspects of the same process. This possibility was tested by calculating correlations between the two groups of test discussed above, in the case of the Chapman Test 1 only the total error score being used. This was because it correlated very highly with all other measures on that test. The correlations obtained between the various scores from the five divergent thinking and three conceptual tests are shown in Table 3.12. As can be seen there, apart from the POCT Non-A score and some of the CT2 scores, all of the conceptual thinking and divergent thinking measures were significantly correlated. However, the signs of these correlations are opposite to expectation. Thus, it was predicted that thinking would be more divergent in those subjects with greater overinclusion; yet both Chapman overinclusion scores correlated *negatively* with the divergent thinking measures.

It will be recalled from the previous section that the conceptual measures tended to correlate with intelligence. In order to clarify the relationships within the data a principal components analysis, with

TABLE 3.12

CORRELATIONS BETWEEN CONCEPTUAL THINKING AND DIVERGENT THINKING TESTS

| | Payne OCT | | Chapman Test 1 | Chapman Test 2 | |
	A responses	Non-A responses	Total errors	Overinclusive errors	Overexclusive errors
Word Association	0·49‡	0·11	−0·37‡	−0·23‡	−0·51‡
Unusual Uses	0·39‡	0·07	−0·27‡	−0·14	−0·30‡
Consequences	0·42‡	0·01	−0·34‡	−0·27‡	−0·42‡
Making Objects	0·38‡	0·09	−0·32‡	−0·15†	−0·32‡
Gottschaldt Figures	0·49‡	0·01	−0·33‡	−0·15†	−0·39‡

† $p < 0.05$.
‡ $p < 0.01$.

In all cases $N = 170$.

Varimax rotation, was therefore carried out. Only one factor with a root greater than one emerged and this accounted for 90·8% of the total variance. All but the POCT Non-A score had their greatest loadings on this factor which would appear to be a general component of intellectual capacity. Divergent thinking would therefore appear to be related to performance on conceptual tests in so far as both are associated with this general factor, part of which is certainly accounted for by intelligence as measured by conventional tests.

Personality and cognitive function

Since personality questionnaires were administered to the twins in the present study (see Chapter 2), it was considered of interest to investigate the relationship between personality and cognitive functioning on the twin sample. There has been a large number of studies of personality in relation to creative abilities, some examining the personality correlates of creativity test performance (Anderson and Cropley, 1966; Barron, 1955) and others investigating the personalities of unusually creative individuals (Barron, 1963; Roe, 1953; Cattell and Drevdahl, 1955). All have found consistent, if somewhat general, relationships. Creative persons have been shown to be more self-sufficient, independent, stable, open to the irrational in themselves, dominant, self-assertive, resourceful, adventurous, radical, and possibly more sensitive and introverted. There is little evidence of a relationship between creativity and neuroticism as a general personality dimension, though it has been suggested that creative people have higher levels of anxiety or tension (Cattell, 1963; Cattell and Butcher, 1968). As previously stated, it has also been suggested that there is an association between psychosis and creativity and it was this supposed relationship that provided part of the interest of the present study. Thus, if, as discussed earlier, divergent and overinclusive thinking are the result of a similar cognitive or attentional style, we might expect both to be associated with similar personality traits.

Exact predictions here are difficult to make, however. Certainly there is agreement if one relies on inferences drawn from the two main theories involved: that trying to explain divergent thinking in terms of cognitive style or that relating over inclusion to attention. Thus,

Silverman (1964), adopting the former view, has argued that the extreme scanning supposedly underlying divergent thinking may be characteristic of the cyclothyme or extravert. Similar cyclothymic and extraverted traits have also been linked to overinclusion and poor selective attention by Claridge (1967). On the other hand, as we have just seen, direct studies of creative persons have suggested that the latter tend to be introverted, rather than extraverted. In view of these uncertainties the present study was regarded as purely exploratory, being confined to a simple examination of the correlations between the various cognitive measures included here and the personality questionnaire scores available on the same subjects and described in the previous chapter.

Considering, first, the association between personality and divergent thinking, Table 3.13 gives the results for those tests where a significant correlation was found. For the most part the correlations were low and the pattern of association different for each divergent thinking test. One consistent finding, however, was that for neuroticism, as measured by the EPI and the 16PF. Eight out of twelve possible correlations here were significant, in all cases the tendency being for neuroticism to correlate negatively with divergent thinking. This might be taken to confirm Cattell's finding that creative people are not more neurotic than the general population. More speculatively it could be said to be in line with the recent suggestion by Claridge, and discussed by him in Chapters 5 and 6, that low neuroticism actually reflects psychotic personality structure; hence providing part of the theoretical link between psychosis and creativity. It is therefore interesting to note in passing that some of the results to be presented by him in Chapter 6 suggest that individuals classified on physiological grounds as of psychotic "nervous type" tend to have higher divergent thinking scores.

Turning to the other second-order personality dimension considered here, namely extraversion, it can be seen from Table 3.13 that significant correlations, where they appeared, were all positive, indicating that extraverts showed greater divergent thinking. However, it should be noted that a large proportion of the correlations here failed to reach significance at all, while the measures of sociability and impulsivity correlated with only one of the divergent thinking tests, namely Making

TABLE 3.13

CORRELATIONS BETWEEN PERSONALITY TESTS AND DIVERGENT THINKING TESTS

	Word Association	Unusual Uses	Consequences	Making Objects	Gottschaldt Figures	Total
EPI						
Neuroticism	−0·16†	−0·22‡		−0·21‡	−0·24‡	−0·25‡
Extraversion				0·21‡		
Sociability				0·20‡		
Impulsivity				0·17†		
16PF						
A (Reserve)	0·24‡		0·15†	0·22‡		0·23‡
B (Intelligence)	0·23‡		0·18†	0·36‡		0·37‡
E (Assertiveness)		0·31‡	0·26‡	0·24‡		0·15†
F (Sobriety)						
G (Expedience)				−0·19†		
H (Shyness)				0·15†		
I (Tender-mindedness)	0·15†	0·19†	0·19†	0·17†	−0·26‡	0·23‡
O (Placidness)		0·16†				
Q1 (Conservativeness)	−0·17†		−0·24‡			
Q3 (Self-conflict)				−0·18†	−0·28‡	−0·18†
Neuroticism		0·16†		−0·16†		−0·16†
Extraversion				−0·16†		
Anxiety	0·15†	0·16†		−0·28‡	−0·18†	0·21‡
Creativity		0·15†				
Foulds Hostility Scale						
Self-criticism	−0·16†			−0·19†	−0·29‡	−0·18†
Delusional guilt					−0·29‡	
Intropunitiveness					−0·32‡	
Direction of hostility				−0·18†	−0·17†	−0·18†
General hostility					−0·25‡	

† *p* < 0.05.   ‡ *p* < 0.01.   In all cases *N* = 170.

Note. Where personality traits are not listed or cells are left blank the correlation failed to reach the 0·05 level of significance.

Objects. Perhaps all that can be concluded is that in this sample, at least, there is little evidence that creativity is associated with introversion. If anything, the opposite is true and to that extent the results can be said to conform to the expectations of the cognitive style and attention theories of divergent thinking discussed earlier.

At the trait level of description, as measured by the first-order factors of the 16PF, only three characteristics seemed to be consistently related to divergent thinking. Factor E showed a positive correlation with five of the measures, indicating that divergent thinkers were more assertive and dominant. They also emerged as more tender-minded (Factor I) and had more undisciplined self-conflict (Factor Q3); though not all of the divergent thinking tests correlated significantly with these two traits.

Finally there were a number of correlations, all negative, between the divergent thinking tests and the various scores from the Foulds Hostility Scale. The most consistently related score was self-criticism, though intropunitiveness also showed three significant correlations with divergent thinking. It seems very likely that the results for the Foulds scale reflect its correlation with neuroticism, reported in the previous chapter. In that case the tendency for divergent thinkers to be less hostile would be in keeping with the fact that they also tend to have lower scores on the 16PF and EPI neuroticism factors.

Compared with the divergent thinking measures the conceptual tests showed few significant correlations with personality (see Table 3.14). The measure most consistently correlated with the personality questionnaires was the A response score from the POCT. It was positively related to intelligence (B), assertiveness (E), and conscientiousness (G) on the 16PF; and negatively with three of the hostility scores. However, as this measure is considered to be independent of overinclusion/overexclusion the pattern of correlations is difficult to interpret. The only findings of interest—and in line with prediction—were the, respectively, positive and negative correlations between the 16PF creativity measure and the Chapman Test 1 error and Chapman Test 2 overexclusion scores. It is also of some interest that the *overinclusion* score of the latter test was positively correlated with the EPI extraversion factor; a result in keeping with the positive correlation between this personality dimension and divergent thinking. Otherwise, however,

TABLE 3.14
CORRELATIONS BETWEEN PERSONALITY TESTS AND CONCEPTUAL THINKING TESTS

	Payne OCT		Chapman Test 1	Chapman Test 2	
	A responses	Non-A responses	Total errors	Overinclusive errors	Overexclusive errors
EPI					
Neuroticism					
Extraversion				0·15†	−0·16†
16PF					
B (Intelligence)	0·30‡		−0·38‡	−0·17†	−0·25‡
E (Assertiveness)	0·23‡				−0·17†
I (Tender-mindedness)					−0·15†
M (Imaginativeness)					
Creativity			0·15†	0·18†	−0·29‡
Foulds Hostility Scale					
Criticism of others	−0·18†				
Extrapunitiveness	−0·16†				
Direction of hostility	−0·16†	−0·17†			

† $p < 0.05$.   In all cases $N = 170$.
‡ $p < 0.01$.
Note: Where personality traits are not listed or cells are left blank the correlation failed to reach the 0·05 level of significance.

there was little to confirm the expectation that overinclusion and divergent thinking would be related to similar personality traits. It is, of course, possible that these rather disappointing results partly reflected the insensitivity of the conceptual thinking tests which were originally designed to detect the gross cognitive disorder found in schizophrenic patients.

Summary and conclusions

It is evident that this chapter has gone far beyond a simple comparison of MZ and DZ twins on cognitive variables. However, as part of the deliberate plan for the project, measures were selected for study not only because of an interest in the genetics of behaviour but also in an endeavour to synthesize various aspects of research concerned with cognitive processes and personality. Looked at from the latter point of view the results were, in a sense, disappointing. Any relationship that might exist between divergent thinking and overinclusion was, in the present data, obscured by the tendency for both groups of measure to share a high common loading on a more general factor of intellectual function. This is not to say that divergent thinking could be considered synonymous with intelligence, as measured by standard tests, since the two were clearly correlated only up to a certain IQ level. Beyond that divergent thinking was less obviously influenced by general intelligence.

There was little evidence that personality was the factor linking over-inclusion and divergent thinking, at least when examined by looking at their respective correlations with questionnaire scores. However, the divergent thinking measures did show a number of relationships with personality which were consistent with the theory underlying our choice of measures; notably positive correlations with extraversion and negative correlations with neuroticism. On the other hand, the correlations themselves were low, indicating that most of the variance was taken up by intellectual rather than personality factors.

Regarding the comparisons of MZ and DZ twins there was certainly evidence that some of the divergent thinking tests were subject to significant genetic determination, though the extent to which this was so seemed to depend on the degree to which a particular measure correlated with intelligence. This was shown by the very clear tendency for the difference between the two types of twin to increase as a function of the relationship between intelligence and divergent thinking. Finally, the results for the conceptual measures did provide some evidence that hereditary factors may be important on tests where the ability to exclude irrelevant stimuli is involved. Again general intelligence tended to cloud the picture, though to a lesser extent than in the case of the divergent thinking tests, and the findings from this part of the study can be considered of some interest in that they help to elucidate the influence of heredity on certain aspects of cognitive function known to be disordered in schizophrenia.

References

ANDERSON, C. C. and CROPLEY, A. J. (1966) Some correlates of originality. *Austral. J. Psychol.* **18**, 218–27.

BAGGERLEY, A. R. (1955) Concept formation and its relation to cognitive variables. *J. gen. Psychol.* **52**, 297–306.

BARRON, F. (1955) The disposition toward originality. *J. abn. soc. Psychol.* **51**, 478–85.

BARRON, F. (1963) *Creativity and Psychological Health.* Van Nostrand, Princeton, N.J.

BLEWETT, D. B. (1954) An experimental study of the inheritance of intelligence. *J. ment. Sci.* **100**, 922–33.

BURT, C. (1962) Critical notice of *Creativity and Intelligence* by Getzels and Jackson. *Brit. J. educ. Psychol.* **32**, 292–8.

BURT, C. (1966) The genetic determination of differences in intelligence: a study of monozygotic twins reared together and apart. *Brit. J. Psychol.* **57**, 137–53.

BUTCHER, H. J. (1970) *Human Intelligence. Its Nature and Assessment.* Methuen, London.

CATTELL, R. B. (1963) The personality and motivation of the researcher from measurements of contemporaries and from biography. In Taylor, C. W. and Barron, F. (Eds.) *Scientific Creativity: its Recognition and Development.* Wiley, New York.

CATTELL, R. B. and BUTCHER, H. J. (1968) *The Prediction of Achievement and Creativity.* Bobbs Merrill, Indianapolis.

CATTELL, R. B. and DREVDAHL, J. E. (1955) A comparison of the personality profile of eminent researchers with that of eminent teachers and administrators and of the general population. *Brit. J. Psychol.* **46**, 248–61.

CHAPMAN, L. J. (1956) Distractability in the conceptual performance of schizophrenics. *J. abn. soc. Psychol.* **53**, 286–91.

CHAPMAN, L. J. (1961) A reinterpretation of some pathological disturbances in conceptual breadth. *J. abn. soc. Psychol.* **62**, 514–19.

CHAPMAN, L. J. and TAYLOR, J. A. (1957) The breadth of deviate concepts used by schizophrenics. *J. abn. soc. Psychol.* **54**, 118–23.

CLARIDGE, G. S. (1967) *Personality and Arousal.* Pergamon, Oxford.

CLARIDGE, G. S. (1972) The schizophrenias as nervous types. *Brit. J. Psychiat.* **121**, 1–17.

DE MILLE, R. and MERRIFIELD, P. R. (1962) Review of *Creativity and Intelligence* by Getzels and Jackson. *Educ. psychol. Measurement* 22, 803–8.

EDWARDS, M. P. and TYLER, L. E. (1965) Intelligence, creativity and achievement in a non-selective public junior high school. *J. educ. Psychol.* 56, 96–99.

ERLENMEYER-KIMLING, L. and JARVIK, L. F. (1963) Genetics and intelligence: a review. *Science* 142, 1477–9.

GARDNER, R. W. (1959) Cognitive control principles and perceptual behaviour. *Bull. Menninger Clinic* 23, 241–8.

GARDNER, R. W. (1961) Cognitive controls of attention deployment as determinants of visual illusions. *J. abn. soc. Psychol.* 62, 120–7.

GARDNER, R. W., HOLZMAN, P. S., KLEIN, G. S., LINTON, H. P. and SPENCE, D. P. (1959) Cognitive control: a study of individual consistencies in cognitive behaviour. *Psychol. Issues* 1, 1–186.

GETZELS, J. W. and JACKSON, P. W. (1962) *Creativity and Intelligence*. Wiley, New York.

GOLDSTEIN, K. (1939) The significance of special mental tests for diagnosis and prognosis in schizophrenia. *Amer. J. Psychiat.* 96, 575–87.

GOTTSCHALDT, K. (1926) Uber den Einfluss der Erfahrung auf die Wahrnehming von Figuren. *Psychol. Forsch.* 8, 261–317.

GUILFORD, J. P. (1967) *The Nature of Human Intelligence*. McGraw-Hill, New York.

HASAN, P. and BUTCHER, H. J. (1966) Creativity and intelligence: a partial replication with Scottish children of Getzels and Jackson's study. *Brit. J. Psychol.* 57, 129–35.

HAWKS, D. V. (1964) The clinical usefulness of some measures of thinking in psychiatric patients. *Brit. J. soc. clin. Psychol.* 3, 186–95.

KLEIN, G. S. (1958) Cognitive control and motivation. In Lindzay, G. (Ed.) *Assessment of Human Motives*. Rinehart, New York.

KRETSCHMER, E. (1931) *The Psychology of Men of Genius*. Kegan Paul, London.

McCONAGHY, N. (1959) The use of an object sorting test in elucidating the hereditary factors in schizophrenia. *J. Neurol. Neurosurg. Psychiat.* 22, 243–6.

McCONAGHY, N. (1960) Modes of abstract thinking and psychosis. *Amer. J. Psychiat.* 117, 106–10.

McCONAGHY, N. (1961) The measurement of inhibitory processes in human higher nervous activity: its relation to allusive thinking and fatigue. *Amer. J. Psychiat.* 118, 125–32.

McCONAGHY, N. and CLANCY, M. (1968) Familial relationships of allusive thinking in University students and their parents. *Brit. J. Psychiat.* 114, 1079–87.

MORE, R. (1966) The relation of intelligence to creativity. *J. Res. in music Educ.* 14, 143–253.

PAYNE, R. W. (1960) Cognitive abnormalities. In Eysenck, H. J. (Ed.) *Handbook of Abnormal Psychology*. Pitman, London.

PAYNE, R. W. (1962) An object classification test as a measure of overinclusive thinking in schizophrenic patients. *Brit. J. soc. clin. Psychol.* 1, 213–21.

PAYNE, R. W. and HEWLETT, J. H. G. (1960) Thought disorder in psychotic patients. In Eysenck, H. J. (Ed.) *Experiments in Personality*. Routledge and Kegan Paul, London.

PHILLIPS, J. E., JACOBSON, N. and TURNER, W. H. J. (1965) Conceptual thinking in schizophrenics and their relatives. *Brit. J. Psychiat.* 111, 823–39.

PRICE, P. H. (1970) Task requirements in tests of schizophrenic overinclusion. *Brit. J. soc. clin. Psychol.* **9**, 60–67.

ROE, A. (1953) A psychological study of eminent psychologists and anthropologists, and a comparison with biological and physical scientists. *Psychol. Monogr.* **67**, No. 2.

SILVERMAN, J. (1964) The problem of attention in research and theory in schizophrenia. *Psychol. Rev.* **71**, 352–64.

SPOTTS, J. and MACKLER, B. (1967) Relationships of field-independence and field-dependence cognitive styles to creative test performance. *Percept. mot. Skills* **24**, 239–68.

STUART, I. R., BRESLOW, A., BRECHNER, S., ILYUS, R. and WOLPOFF, M. (1965) The question of constitutional influence on perceptual style. *Percept. mot. Skills* **20**, 419–20.

THURSTONE, T. G., THURSTONE, U. and STRANDSKOW, H. H. (1955) *A Psychological Study of Twins.* Psychometric Lab. University of North Carolina Report No. 4.

TORRANCE, E. P. (1965) *Rewarding Creative Behaviour.* Prentice Hall, Englewood Cliffs, N.J.

VANDENBERG, S. G. (1962) The hereditary abilities study: hereditary components in a psychological test battery. *Amer. J. hum. Genet.* **14**, 220–37.

VANDENBERG, S. G. (1965) Multivariate analysis of twin differences. In Vandenberg, S. G. (Ed.) *Methods and Goals in Human Behaviour Genetics.* Academic Press, New York.

VANDENBERG, S. G. (1966) Contributions of twin research to psychology. *Psychol. Bull.* **66**, 329–52.

VANDENBERG, S. G. (1967) Hereditary factors in psychological variables in man, with special emphasis on cognition. In Spuhler, J. N. (Ed.) *Genetic Diversity and Human Behaviour.* Aldine Publ. Co., Chicago.

WALLACH, M. and KOGAN, N. (1965) A new look at the creativity-intelligence distinction. *J. Personal.* **33**, 348–69.

WITKIN, H. A., DYK, R. B., FATERSON, H. F., GOODENOUGH, D. R. and KARP, S. A. (1962) *Psychological Differentiation.* Wiley, New York.

YAMAMOTO, K. (1964) Threshold of intelligence in academic achievement of highly creative students. *J. exper. Educ.* **32**, 401–4.

CHAPTER 4

PHYSIOLOGICAL MEASURES
IN TWINS

By W. I. HUME

Introduction

In his introduction to twin studies, Mittler (1971) says "psychologists have tended to neglect biological aspects of behaviour" and that "this neglect has been particularly unfortunate in twins studies, since many biological characteristics lend themselves to much more precise and reliable measurement than the traditional measures of intelligence and personality". As we shall see later in this chapter, that statement is something of an oversimplification in that some physiological measures at least leave a great deal to be desired in terms of reliability (see also Block, 1967).

The other important aspect of measurement, that of validity, is also relevant but is rarely considered. It may well be that a person's pulse beat is a valid and reliable measure of his heart rate and that it appears to be determined by genetic factors. But such an observation is of limited significance unless it can be put into the context of the functioning organism and the result interpreted with reference to some framework which has implications for the behaviour of the organism outside the experimental situation. In the field of psychophysiology there is a frequent failure to do so. For example, Young and Fenton (1971) state that the EEG alpha-blocking effect is well-known, although "its exact significance remains unknown", and then without further elaboration go on to demonstrate the action of a possible genetic component. Without reference to some wider body of theory such data are of limited interest.

Psychophysiological measures are, of course, notoriously variable in the way in which they correlate with each other and with other, behavioural, indices that may provide them with psychological significance. For example, it has long been assumed that behavioural—and subjective—anxiety is associated with an increase in physiological, especially autonomic, activity. The experimental evidence on this point is, however, far from unanimous (Hume, 1972a) and the use of physiological measures as indices of psychological states must still be regarded with caution. Consequently, even if it is demonstrated that constitutional factors affect physiological activity, this does not prove that "anxiety" is also determined by such factors. Only where there are firmly established links between physiology and behaviour can we infer the role of genetic factors in determining behaviour from a knowledge of their control over the supposedly more objective physiological measures.

When the opportunity to study the present group of twins arose it was taken up as much with a view to obtaining information from a sample of "normal" people as to looking at the possible influence of genetic factors on some physiological measures. The former aspect of the work has been discussed in detail elsewhere (Hume, 1970, 1972b), the present account being confined mainly to the twin comparisons.

A selective review of the literature

Before presenting our own twin data the findings of some other workers in this area will be reviewed. Lamentably few of these studies can be regarded with any degree of credibility. Some have used only MZ twins, some have mixed normal and patient subjects, others adults and children while most have studied small samples. In reviewing the past literature we shall consider the various studies in groups according to the measures used.

Cardiovascular measures

Barcal *et al.* (1969) studied blood pressure in thirty-nine pairs of MZ and fifty-one pairs of DZ twins. They found small values of h^2

for casual blood pressure readings, but higher values in a small group studied at intervals throughout the day, the several readings being averaged. Supporting these results Downie *et al.* (1969) found no significant difference between the mean intra-pair variance for fifty MZ and thirty-one DZ pairs using a single casual reading. On the other hand, Osborne *et al.* (1963) did find significant differences for casual blood pressure in thirty-four MZ and nineteen DZ pairs; while Shapiro *et al.* (1968) found twelve MZ pairs to be more alike in their blood pressure response to pain than twelve DZ pairs. Kryshova *et al.* (1962) observed that the blood pressure response to cold stimuli was very similar for both members of an MZ pair. They studied eleven MZ pairs but only two DZ pairs and present no statistical analysis of their results. Jost and Sontag (1944) showed the intrapair differences in resting pulse pressure to be significantly less in a small group of MZ twins than in pairs of sibs or unrelated control pairs. Finally, after reviewing familial studies, Miall *et al.* (1967) decided that blood pressure was multifactorially determined and that, not surprisingly, there was an interaction between genetic and environmental factors, the former probably being more important. A similar conclusion was reached much earlier by Stocks (1930).

Investigations of heart rate have also shown the possible importance of genetic factors. Shapiro *et al.* (1968) found MZ twins to be more alike than DZs for both heart rate level and response to mildly stressful stimuli. Mathers *et al.* (1961) observed significant F-ratios for inter/intrapair variances in both MZ and DZ twins, using resting heart rate as their measure. Jost and Sontag (1944) found no differences in intrapair variance comparing MZ twins and pairs of sibs for resting heart rate. Lader and Wing (1966), however, reported, in a study of the habituation of physiological responses, that there was a significant difference in the intraclass correlations of eleven MZ and eleven DZ twins when the level of heart rate at the end of the experiment was taken as a measure. Block (1967) also found a significant intraclass correlation for heart rate level, both resting and stimulus-induced, in a group of twenty-one MZ pairs; though he did not study a DZ sample. Finally, Vandenberg *et al.* (1965), in groups of twenty-two MZ and sixteen DZ pairs, found significant DZ/MZ within-pair variance ratios for heart rate response to the most intense pair of five arousing stimuli.

Electrodermal measures

Lader and Wing (1966) in the study already referred to found significant differences in the intraclass correlations of MZ and DZ twins using an index of the habituation rate of the skin conductance response and also the frequency of spontaneous skin conductance fluctuations occurring during the experiment. Rachman (1960), however, obtained a non-significant correlation from seven MZ twins for a measure of the habituation rate of the skin resistance response; though he did find a highly significant value for the latency of the response. Vandenberg *et al.* (1965) found non-significant values of the DZ/MZ within-pair variance ratios using skin resistance response to five different types of stimulus. Block (1967) observed very high intraclass correlations for skin resistance level in MZ twins, while Jost and Sontag (1944) found MZ twins to be more alike than sibling pairs on a measure of resting skin resistance level.

EEG measures

Most of the EEG studies in twins have involved a visual inspection of the whole EEG record, followed by a subjective estimate of the similarities between the records of twin pair members. This is a procedure not renowned for its reliability. Two studies are worthy of mention here as they used defined aspects of the EEG activity. Dustman and Beck (1965) looked at the visual evoked response in twelve MZ and eleven DZ pairs of twin children and found that members of the MZ pairs were significantly more alike than members of the DZ pairs. An interesting observation was that sometimes the variability between twins on one occasion was less than the variability between occasions of testing for one twin. This would suggest that the variability of visual evoked response is an important parameter and worthy of study in its own right. The second EEG study of interest has already been mentioned, that by Young and Fenton (1971). They investigated the habituation of the EEG alpha blocking response with repeated stimulation and found significant intraclass correlations in seventeen MZ pairs. Although the latter were not significantly different from a group of fifteen DZ pairs, they did differ from a sample of thirty pairs of unrelated control subjects.

Other measures

Some less popular psychophysiological measures have been investigated in a few twin studies. For example, Lader and Wing (1966) found that the intraclass correlations for integrated forearm extensor muscle activity were low in both MZ and DZ twin groups. Vandenberg *et al.* (1965) showed a closer concordance in MZ twins on a measure of respiratory response to intense stimuli, while Block (1967) found significant, though low, intraclass correlation values for respiratory period in MZ pairs. Jost and Sontag (1944), however, found the intrapair differences on this measure to be similar in both MZ twins and sibling pairs, while neither of these groups differed from unrelated control pairs. These authors did find that MZ twins were more alike than pairs of sibs on measures of salivation and vasomotor persistence. They also found that the average correlation between pairs of subjects for seven autonomic variables was greater in MZ twins than in sibs. This suggests that there might be a genetic component in the determination of overall levels of physiological activity, a conclusion partly confirmed by Jost and Sontag's finding that a measure of "autonomic balance", derived from the factor analytic work of Wenger (Wenger and Ellington, 1943), was more similar in pairs of MZ twins than in sibs or in unrelated controls. Their work is interesting in that they are the only workers to have investigated combined measures of general physiological activity, rather than single measures. It is true that their statistical analyses are somewhat primitive by contemporary standards and their groups rather unbalanced. Thus, they used sixteen pairs of MZ twins, fifty-four pairs of sibs, and 1025 pairs of unrelated subjects, all children; these being the combined samples for three separate investigations. However, their approach would seem to be potentially more valid than the traditional procedure of examining single measures.

Discussion

The studies mentioned above illustrate the variable nature of the information available in this area. Where a measure has been studied by more than one investigator the results tend to be contradictory. The reasons for this are unclear, though there are three possible explanations. First, physiological activity depends critically on the circumstances under which it is measured and no two experiments are ever exactly identical. Consequently a proportion of the variance of any measure will be due to specific environmental factors, which could well account for the differences observed. Secondly, the choice of an index of physiological activity is still a very arbitrary matter and could affect results. For example, in their study of electrodermal activity Lader and Wing (1966) used an index of response in terms of skin conductance, whereas Rachman (1960) used skin resistance and obtained different results. This question of measurement will be discussed further later in the chapter. Thirdly, the index of twin similarity used by different investigators varies considerably, some using intraclass correlations, for example, while others have preferred within-pair variance comparisons.

If any conclusion can be drawn from the literature reviewed it is that cardiovascular measures seem to show the possible effects of genetic factors more strongly than other indices; while from the sparse evidence on the EEG it would appear that this is an area worth exploring further, using more valid techniques than those adopted in most studies hitherto. Finally, it would seem important to examine composite groups of measures, perhaps representing common physiological systems, rather than individual indices. It was with this consideration particularly in mind that the study reported in the following section was planned.

The present study

The psychophysiological measures chosen for study here were selected in order to test out some hypotheses concerning the "arousal" concept (Duffy, 1962), the experiment actually forming part of a larger investigation of normal and psychiatric subjects reported elsewhere (Hume, 1970). Only relevant procedural details will therefore be described here.

As reported in Chapter 1, after their arrival at the department twin members were allocated to the morning or afternoon sessions for the physiological or personality and cognitive test batteries, the twins changing places after lunch. To reduce any systematic bias in the choice of twin with respect to order of testing the eldest twin underwent the physiological procedures first on half the occasions.

After being shown the laboratory the subject was asked if he wished

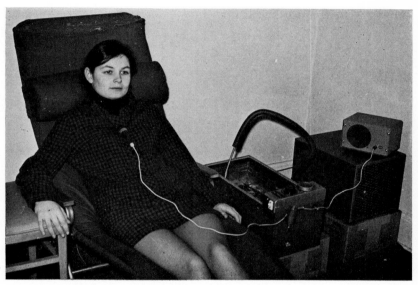

PLATE 1. Conditions of psychophysiological measurement illustrated, showing the "Relaxator" sun lounger on which the subject was seated, the cold pressor bath and the intercom system used for communication between the recording and test rooms

to visit the toilet as he would not be able to do so for the following hour or so. He then reclined on a "Relaxator" sun lounger (see Plate 1) and the recording electrodes were attached; their purpose being explained at each stage. Two perceptual tests—the spiral after-effect and two-flash threshold—which were subsequently to be used were demonstrated, the subject having a trial run on each. In addition to these measures four physiological variables were monitored: palmar skin potential, finger pulse volume, heart rate, and occipital EEG. This was done in an air-conditioned, sound-attenuated laboratory, the temperature being $20°C \pm 1°C$ and the humidity $40\% \pm 5\%$. The recording apparatus, a Grass Model 5 Polygraph, was in the room adjacent to the subject, who at all times could communicate with the experimenter either directly or via a microphone slung round his neck.

Techniques of measurement

Skin potential (SP). This is an electrodermal measure, which, centrally, is under sympathetic control (Hume, 1966). At the time it was preferred to the more popular resistance-derived measures as these are markedly influenced by the effects of non-nervous peripheral factors and by the techniques of measurement (e.g. Wenger, 1962). Recent evidence, however, indicates that skin potential too may be affected by non-nervous factors to a degree greater than was previously thought (Christie and Venables, 1971). Recording in the present instance was via Ag/AgCl button electrodes, 9·5 mm diameter, with 5% KCl solution in agar–agar as the electrolyte (Venables and Sayer, 1963). The indifferent electrode was placed on an abraded site on the ventral surface of the right forearm, at the level of the wrist, with the active electrode on the palmar surface of the proximal segment of the index finger of the right hand. Each electrode pair was checked immediately before use and rejected if there was a standing potential difference of more than 0·5 mV, or a drift value of greater than 0·1 mV/hr.

Finger pulse volume (FPV). This measure represents the amplitude of the volume change of a finger tip with each heart stroke. It is under sympathetic control (Shepherd, 1963), the peripheral transmitter being noradrenaline (Lader and Montagu, 1962). Given a constant physical posture, finger pulse volume is linearly related to the rate of blood flow through the finger within an individual (Zweifler *et al.*, 1967). Recording here was via a CdS photocell and a light source attached to the palmar surface of the distal segment of the middle finger of the right hand, using a Velcro band.

Heart rate (*HR*). The output of the finger pulse volume amplifier was fed into a cardiotachometer which gave a beat-by-beat write-out of the heart period. This was translated into a measure of rate, using a conversion table.

EEG alpha activity (*alpha*). Although the physiological basis of this measure is unclear, it has been shown to be related to behavioural arousal (Lindsley, 1952) and to activity in both sides of the ANS (Gellhorn, 1967). Measurement here was with Ag button electrodes with 5% KCl in agar–agar as the electrolyte. One electrode was placed on the midline, just above the occiput, and the other 3 cm vertically above the right ear. The earth electrode was on an abraded site on the ventral surface of the right forearm. To extract the alpha band of frequencies the output of the Grass pre-amplifier was passed through a band-pass filter (Barr and Stroud, Anniesland, Glasgow) with characteristics such that frequencies outwith the range 6·5 to 14·5 Hz were attenuated by at least 12 dB. This meant that any recorded signal with an amplitude at source of greater than 5 μV almost certainly came from within this band. The filter attenuated the original signal somewhat, necessitating a rather high gain setting.

Two-flash threshold (*TFT*). This is the threshold of fusion for pairs of brief light flashes. Pairs of square wave flashes, each of 5 msec duration, were presented at 6-sec intervals through a circular aperture subtending an angle of 1° 48′ at the eye. The vacuum light source had a screen decay time of 5 μsec and a phosphor characteristic with a maximum light output at 5600 Å. The interflash interval was varied in steps of 2 msec, the method of limits being used to determine the threshold of fusion (Hume and Claridge, 1965). Two increasing and two decreasing thresholds were determined alternately, the TFT being the mean of these four. The reliability, defined as the correlation between the mean of the first pair of increasing and decreasing thresholds and the mean of the second pair, was 0·96 for a sample of forty subjects.

Spiral after-effect (SAE). This is the duration of the movement after-effect observed following fixation of a rotating Archimedes spiral (Holland, 1965). A four-throw spiral, subtending an angle of 8° 22′ at the eye, rotating at 73 rpm and illuminated by two 60 watt lights, was used, the subject fixating the centre and reporting when all movement had stopped, following a 60-sec rotation period. The measure referred to later as SAE 1 was the mean of two determinations, separated by a 60-sec rest period. The reliability, defined as the correlation between these two determinations, was 0·80 for a sample of seventy-six subjects.

The testing session, then, involved the continuous monitoring of the four physiological variables and the periodic administration of the two perceptual tests just described. In addition, the effect of two physiological stressors was measured, namely an habituation procedure and the cold pressor test. The actual schedule followed during testing is shown in Table 4.1. This was identical for all subjects, except that some

TABLE 4.1
EXPERIMENTAL PROCEDURES

1	*Rest 1.* Eyes closed, no stimulation.	5 min
2	*Alpha blocking.* 60 sec fixation of rotating spiral followed by immediate closing of eyes for at least 90 sec. Repeated 30 sec after eyes were opened.	6 min
3	*TFT 1.* Two-flash threshold determination.	3–5 min
4	*SAE 1a.* Spiral after-effect determination.	2 min
5	*Rest 2.*	3 min
6	*SAE 1b.*	2 min
7	*Habituation.* Twenty 1000 Hz tones of 1 sec duration, intensity 95 db above a 2×10^{-4} dynes/cm^2 threshold, presented randomly through earphones from a tape-recorder, at intervals of between 20 to 50 sec.	13 min
8	*Cold Pressor.* The subject placed hand in a bath of water, temperature 4°C for 60 sec. On removal of hand, subject relaxed with eyes closed for at least 3 min.	8 min
9	*TFT 2.*	3–5 min
10	*SAE 2.*	2 min
11	*Rest 3.*	3 min

individuals were not involved in the second determination of the two-flash threshold and spiral after-effect. In those cases Rest 3 followed the cold pressor procedure.

Data reduction

In order to reduce the large amount of data available to a manageable size for statistical analysis certain measures were extracted. Those with skewed or irregular distributions were normalized using an appropriate transformation. Each measure, with a brief description of its derivation, is given below.

Alpha 1. Alpha index for the last 60 sec of Rest 1. Alpha index was taken as the percent time during which signals of amplitude greater than 5 μV were recorded. Measurement was by eye, using a transparent template to define amplitude limits and a pair of dividers as a cumulative store. The reliability of this method was 0·98 using two independent scorers and thirty-nine 1 min samples of record.

Alpha 2. As alpha 1 for Rest 3.

Alpha frequency. Mean alpha frequency of nine 1-sec samples, three from each of the rest periods.

Alpha block. Duration of the delay in the return of alpha activity after spiral fixation which was followed by the eyes being closed. The phenomenon is illustrated in Fig. 4.1. The measure of blocking was derived by dividing the eyes-closed period into thirty 3-sec segments. Blocking was considered to have stopped when (a) two successive segments contained at least 50% alpha activity of the same amplitude as the maximum occurring during the total 90-sec eye-closed period; or (h) one segment contained 100% alpha of this amplitude. The mean of two trials was taken as the measure of alpha block. The reliability of scoring was 0·99 for a sample of thirty trials. The reliability of the test, defined as the correlation between the scores for the two trials, was 0·66 for a sample of eighty subjects.

Alpha spirals. The sum of alpha indices for the four spiral fixation periods; i.e. with eyes open.

(a)
Normal

eyes closed

(b)
After fixating spiral

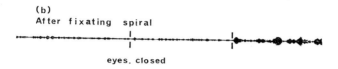

eyes. closed

Alpha blocking after spiral fixation

FIG. 4.1. Example of the alpha blocking response induced by spiral fixation; comparing (a) the rapid return of alpha following normal closing of the eyes and (b) delayed return of alpha when the eyes are closed after previous visual stimulation.

TFT 1. Mean of two increasing and two decreasing two-flash threshold determinations.
TFT 2. As for TFT 1.
SAE 1. Mean of two estimates of the spiral after-effect.
SAE 2. Single estimate of the spiral after-effect.
FPV 1. Mean amplitude of six finger pulse volume samples taken at 10-sec intervals during the last 60 sec of Rest 1. A sample was taken as the mean amplitude of five successive deflections. In order to make comparisons across individuals, possible raw scores were converted to range-corrected form (Lykken *et al.*, 1966), where each individual value is expressed as a percentage of the total range of values observed in a given subject, referred to his maximum value as an origin. Thus

$$\text{FPV}_{corrected} = \frac{\text{FPV}_{max} - \text{FPV}_{raw}}{\text{FPV}_{max} - \text{FPV}_{min}} \times 100.$$

FPV 2. As FPV 1 for Rest 3.

FPV orienting response (OR). Magnitude of vasoconstriction occurring within ten heart beats from the first habituation stimulus.

FPV cold pressor response (CPR). Magnitude of response to the cold pressor procedure, being the difference between initial level and minimum level after immersion.

FPV CP recovery. Time elapsing before level returned to, or overshot, the initial level after immersion in the cold pressor bath. Samples were taken at 20-sec intervals and recovery was judged not to have occurred unless two successive samples were at or beyond the initial level.

SP 1. Mean of six samples of skin potential level taken at 10-sec intervals during the last 60 sec of Rest 1.

SP 2. As SP 1 for Rest 3.

SP orienting response (OR). Magnitude of the response to the first habituation stimulus. The skin potential response can be uniphasic positive or negative, or biphasic. The sum of both components, where they occurred, was used here. The principle of this scoring method is illustrated in Fig. 4.2, which shows the general form of the orienting response.

SP cold pressor response (CPR). The difference between initial level and maximum level after immersion in the cold pressor bath.

SP CP recovery. As FPV CP recovery.

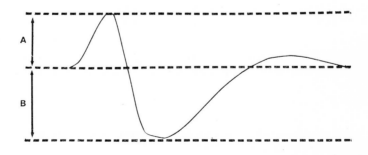

SCHEMATIC BIPHASIC ORIENTING RESPONSE

Fɪɢ. 4.2. Schematic diagram illustrating the biphasic nature of the orienting response to a novel stimulus.

Habituation slope. The slope of the regression of skin potential responses on log stimulus number for the first ten stimuli of the habituation procedure, corrected for intercept value (Montagu, 1963). Figure 4.3 shows the group data and illustrates the general habituation effect.

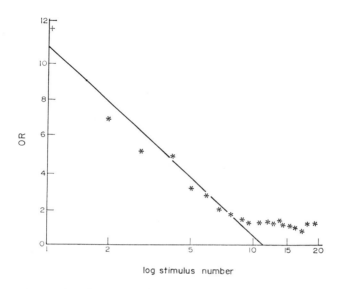

log stimulus number

FIG. 4.3. Diagram, based on group data, showing the habituation of the orienting (skin potential) response following repeatedly presented tone stimuli.

Spontaneous $(R + S)$. Number of spontaneous skin potential fluctuations during the three rest periods and the four spiral fixation periods. A spontaneous fluctuation was defined as a change in level of at least 0·1 mV which began to return to the pre-change level within 5 sec and which occurred in the absence of any apparent change in external stimulation.

Spontaneous (Habituation). Number of spontaneous skin potential fluctuations during the period of the first ten habituation stimuli.

HR 1. Number of heart beats in the last 60 sec of Rest 1.

HR 2. As HR 1 for Rest 3.

HR orienting response (OR). As SP orienting response. The waveform of the heart rate response was variable and it is probable that two successive components were operating. The measure used was represented by A + B in Fig. 4.2, an index recommended by Lang and Hnatiow (1962).

HR cold pressor response (CPR). As SP CPR, the samples of heart rate used in this instance being the mean of five successive beats.

HR CP recovery. As FPV CP recovery.

Results

Raw measures. In this section we shall consider the results of comparing the MZ and DZ twins samples on the individual measures described above; prior, that is, to examining some derived indices which attempt to combine the raw data in possibly more meaningful ways. In doing so it should be borne in mind that none of the measures can be regarded as reflecting any relatively unvarying characteristic of the individual in the same sense that, for example, intelligence test or personality inventory scores can. To illustrate this point it may be mentioned that one subject's heart rate varied between 55 and 130 bpm during the 60 min of the experiment; while virtually all of the subjects were more relaxed at the end of the procedures than at the beginning. It would thus be misleading to ask questions such as "Is heart rate affected by hereditary factors?" A more proper enquiry would be "Is a person's reaction to this situation, as reflected in his heart rate, affected by hereditary factors?" The indices used here may be regarded as a useful basis for comparing twin samples only to the extent that they represent different individuals' reactions to a relatively standard experimental situation.

In order to compare the similarities between members of MZ and DZ pairs it is first necessary to demonstrate that the samples of the two types of twin were most probably drawn from the same population. Means and standard deviations for the twenty-seven measures described above were therefore calculated for each group separately. There were in fact no significant differences between the groups on any measure.

Intraclass correlations are given in Table 4.2, together with the F-ratios comparing the within-pair variances for the two types of twin. It

TABLE 4.2

RAW PSYCHOPHYSIOLOGICAL MEASURES

INTRACLASS CORRELATIONS AND F-RATIOS

Variable	MZ		DZ		F
	n	r_I	n	r_I	
Alpha 1	38	0·69‡	43	0·42‡	1·89†
Alpha 2	36	0·60‡	42	0·23	1·67
Alpha frequency	36	0·75‡	41	0·40‡	2·19†
Alpha blocking	39	0·22	42	0·39‡	0·69
Alpha spirals	39	0·21	43	0·47‡	0·70
TFT 1	40	0·32†	46	0·17	1·26
TFT 2	17	0·52†	30	0·48‡	1·04
SAE 1	43	0·02	51	0·27†	0·82
SAE 2	19	0·29	34	0·21	0·98
FPV 1	29	0·19	36	0·10	1·28
FPV 2	28	0·51‡	36	0·19	1·50
FPV OR	23	0·17	34	−0·15	1·76
FPV CPR	28	0·54†	35	0·18	2·09†
FPV CP recovery	28	−0·08	35	−0·05	0·40
SP 1	41	0·37†	48	0·10	1·17
SP 2	40	0·19	47	0·16	1·15
SP OR	35	0·36†	44	0·12	1·10
SP CPR	40	0·54‡	46	0·48‡	2·51‡
SP CP recovery	40	0·29†	46	0·11	1·36
Habituation slope	34	0·44‡	44	0·24	2·01†
Spont. (R + S)	41	0·32†	48	0·25	0·95
Spont. (Habituation)	35	0·19	44	0·12	0·96
HR 1	37	0·67‡	46	0·33†	3·91‡
HR 2	35	0·65‡	45	0·44‡	2·56‡
HR OR	23	0·39†	37	0·42‡	1·89†
HR CPR	26	0·41†	38	0·39†	1·27
HR CP recovery	26	0·11	38	0·21	0·71

† $p < 0.05$.   ‡ $p < 0.01$.

can be seen that, for the *level* measures, during both rest periods alpha and heart rate have values of r_I in excess of 0·60 for MZ twins, while the respective values for DZ twins are less than 0·44. In both cases the

F-ratios confirm that MZ twins are more alike than DZ twins, suggesting that genetic factors may be important here. For other measures of level the evidence is less clear-cut, neither finger pulse volume nor skin potential showing a difference between the two types of twin.

Turning to the measures of *response*, none of the r_1 values for the orienting indices exceeded 0·42, though the F values for the habituation rate and heart rate orienting response were significant, as were those for the skin potential and finger pulse volume cold pressor responses. However, none of the F-ratios for the recovery measures was significant and the intraclass correlations were uniformly low. In general, there would seem to be some evidence of a genetic influence on certain measures of what may be considered to be sympathetic responsiveness.

As shown in Table 4.2, the two perceptual tests yielded no significant differences between the MZ and DZ samples, though in both types of twin the intraclass correlations were higher for the two-flash threshold than for the spiral after-effect, a fact which may reflect the former's greater reliability of measurement. Of the raw measures, then, evidence for a significant effect of genetic factors seemed to be confined to heart rate and alpha activity recorded at rest and to some indices of sympathetic change under stress.

Factor score measures. It was a general assumption of the theoretical position adopted here that it should be possible to combine raw data such as that just described so that groups of measures can be taken to represent the activity of different physiological systems. The appropriate statistic to use here is some form of factor analysis, so that all those measures behaving in a similar way can be combined into a single factor. A more reliable comparison of MZ and DZ twins should then be possible, using weighted factor scores derived from each factor. Previous studies employing this approach, while using different techniques and different measures, have demonstrated, as one might expect, that more than dimension is required to describe physiological data such as that gathered in the present study. It may be anticipated, therefore, that comparisons between MZ and DZ twin samples can be made on several components of physiological activity.

The present data could have been analysed in two ways. First, the morning and afternoon groups could have been subjected to separate analyses. If the two solutions were different, one would not be justified in taking either as representative of the "true" state of affairs with respect to stable physiological systems underlying the raw data. The second method of analysis would have been to combine the two groups, treating the total sample as a homogeneous whole. This has the apparent disadvantage of averaging out subtle variations between the groups; though, on the other hand, it could be argued that the method allows the extraction of general physiological parameters underlying the behaviour of all of the subjects.

Both approaches were, in fact, used with the twin data. Separate analyses of the morning and afternoon sessions did reveal certain differences which have been discussed in detail elsewhere (Hume, 1970). For the purposes of this presentation, however, the discussion is confined to results obtained from analysing the combined data from both the morning and afternoon sessions. Data for 128 subjects were subjected to a principal components analysis with unities in the diagonal, twenty-one of the variables described in the previous section being included. Variables excluded were not retained either because values were not available for certain subjects (TFT 2 and SAE 2) or because there were very high correlations between measures of a similar type. The latter was true of measures such as Alpha 1 and Alpha 2, FPV 1 and FPV 2 and so on. Only one, the first, estimate was used in the principal components analysis. From this analysis seven components whose latent roots exceeded unity were extracted. The loadings and latent roots for these components are shown in Table 4.3.

Inspection of the table suggests that three or four of the components make some sort of physiological sense. The first component appears to represent autonomic level, though a paradoxical finding is the tendency for a high frequency of skin potential spontaneous fluctuations to be associated with *low* autonomic level. Most previous research, using skin resistance, has observed the opposite relationship (Burch and Greiner, 1960; Lader and Wing, 1966), though there is some evidence that skin potential does not behave in the same way as the exogenous electrodermal equivalent. Component 2 is made up of sympathetic response measures only; while the third factor is clearly an EEG component, the heart rate loading here perhaps reflecting the close relationship suggested between cortical and cardiovascular events (Gellhorn, 1967). Com-

TABLE 4.3

FACTOR LOADINGS FOR THE FIRST SEVEN PRINCIPAL COMPONENTS

	1	2	3	4	5	6	7
Alpha	−0·08	0·04	−0·80	0·03	−0·12	−0·04	0·14
Alpha frequency	0·07	−0·04	0·31	−0·01	0·43	−0·57	−0·27
Alpha blocking	−0·05	0·02	0·61	0·18	0·17	0·24	0·37
Alpha spirals	−0·20	0·01	−0·76	−0·06	0·00	−0·09	−0·15
TFT	−0·01	0·02	−0·06	0·23	0·62	0·37	0·05
SAE	0·28	0·11	0·17	0·18	−0·50	0·14	0·13
FPV	−0·69	0·17	0·08	0·05	0·07	−0·01	−0·14
FPV OR	0·53	−0·28	0·01	0·09	0·14	−0·31	−0·21
FPV CPR	0·76	−0·05	−0·08	0·06	0·21	−0·21	0·12
FPV CP recovery	0·33	0·08	−0·12	0·38	−0·07	−0·39	0·19
SP	−0·54	−0·14	0·14	−0·21	−0·09	0·06	−0·09
SP OR	0·14	−0·81	0·11	0·11	−0·09	0·19	−0·18
SP CPR	0·03	−0·59	−0·09	−0·05	−0·20	−0·13	0·33
SP CP recovery	−0·36	−0·40	0·18	−0·18	−0·16	−0·40	0·47
Habituation	0·08	−0·80	0·10	0·26	−0·05	0·18	−0·16
Spont. (R + S)	0·59	0·20	0·15	−0·57	−0·08	0·22	−0·11
Spont. (Habituation)	0·48	0·16	0·07	−0·65	−0·18	0·11	−0·08
HR	−0·31	0·19	0·44	−0·31	−0·18	−0·35	−0·24
HR OR	−0·21	−0·41	−0·09	−0·28	−0·31	0·05	−0·40
HR CPR	−0·11	−0·24	−0·18	−0·59	0·26	−0·05	0·35
HR CP recovery	−0·03	0·32	0·12	0·43	−0·52	−0·08	0·02
Latent root	2·75	2·36	2·12	1·89	1·53	1·29	1·15

ponents 4 and 5 are difficult to interpret, though the latter could represent some aspect of perceptual efficiency. No other component has loadings in excess of 0·4 on more than three variables and consequently will not be considered further here.

In order to arrive at a more stable solution and define the factors more clearly the first five components were rotated to orthogonal simple structure by the Varimax method, the minimum angle of rotation being 1°. Table 4.4 gives the Varimax loadings, while Table 4.5 lists those variables with loadings exceeding 0·4 on the first four factors.

Factor 1 is now clearly an autonomic level factor and bears a certain similarity to that of "autonomic balance" described by Wenger (1948). Factor 2 represents autonomic, particularly sympathetic, responsiveness and is similar to Freeman and Katzoff's (1942) factor of "arousal".

TABLE 4.4
VARIMAX FACTOR LOADINGS

	1	2	3	4	5
Alpha	0·09	0·06	−0·80	0·12	0·02
Alpha frequency	0·09	0·07	0·41	0·06	0·32
Alpha blocking	−0·07	0·04	0·64	0·15	−0·05
Alpha spirals	−0·02	0·06	−0·75	0·14	0·17
TFT	0·24	0·19	0·13	0·39	0·41
SAE	0·15	−0·06	0·09	−0·18	−0·58
FPV	−0·58	0·20	0·01	0·37	0·05
FPV OR	0·54	−0·25	0·13	−0·11	0·10
FPV CPR	0·75	−0·01	0·07	−0·23	0·11
FPV CP recovery	0·43	0·06	−0·06	0·13	−0·26
SP	−0·55	−0·09	0·07	0·12	0·24
SP OR	0·16	−0·81	0·13	0·07	0·04
SP CPR	0·01	−0·61	−0·13	−0·03	0·01
SP CP recovery	−0·44	−0·42	0·08	0·00	0·05
Habituation	0·18	−0·78	0·14	0·23	0·02
Spont. (R + S)	0·23	0·14	0·12	−0·81	0·06
Spont. (Habituation)	0·10	0·08	0·00	−0·83	0·04
HR	−0·54	0·12	0·30	−0·23	−0·11
HR OR	−0·32	−0·47	−0·21	−0·16	0·01
HR CPR	−0·20	−0·14	−0·18	−0·29	0·58
HR CP recovery	−0·03	0·16	0·02	0·14	−0·73
Latent root	2·52	2·30	2·09	2·06	1·68

TABLE 4.5
VARIABLES WITH LOADINGS IN EXCESS OF 0·40 ON VARIMAX FACTORS

Factor 1	Factor 2	Factor 3	Factor 4
FPV⁻	SP OR⁻	Alpha⁻	Spont. (R + S)⁻
SP⁻	SP Habituation⁻	Alpha spirals⁻	Spont. (Habituation)⁻
HR⁻	HR OR⁻	Alpha frequency⁺	
FPV OR⁺	SP CPR⁻	Alpha blocking⁺	
FPV CPR⁺	SP CP recoverv⁻		
FPV CP recovery⁺			
SP CP recovery⁻			

Both of these factors resemble those described by Mefferd and by Joyce (in Cattell, 1966) after a review of intra- and inter-individual analyses. They claim that two factors appear consistently in different studies, Joyce calling them "general autonomic level" and "motor discharge". Our Factor 3 is an EEG component similar to those found by Nebylitsyn (Gray, 1967), Claridge (1967) and Pawlik and Cattell (1965). Factor 4 isolates spontaneous skin potential activity and has not been described before because this variable has not previously been included in this kind of analysis. Factor 5 cannot be interpreted since it contains the residue of the principal components not taken up in the first four Varimax factors.

The factors described seem, then, to represent identifiable aspects of physiological activity. They are more meaningful than the raw measures in that they represent the common variance between different parameters and any error variance due to measurement techniques, peripheral mechanisms, or patterning phenomena (Lacey, 1967) can be assumed to have been minimized. Strictly speaking, of course, the factors should receive some external validation and check on their stability before they are accepted as meaningful. However, the present study was not designed to investigate either stability or external validity and the appropriate information is not available. One may perhaps take the similarity of Factors 1, 2, and 3 to those found by others, together with their reasonable physiological interpretation, as being presumptive evidence of their stability and validity in a wider context.

With this in mind, factor scores derived from the first four components were calculated for each subject and a comparison made, using these measures, between the MZ and DZ samples. The results of this analysis are shown in Table 4.6. It can be seen that all four intraclass correlations are significant in MZ twins, while in DZ twins only two—those for Factors 2 and 3—are significant. In all cases the values of r_1 are higher in the MZ than in the DZ pairs, though only marginally so for Factor 2. Considering the F-ratios for the within-pair variance comparisons it can be seen that the clearest evidence for a significant contribution of genetic factors occurred in the case of Factor 1— autonomic balance—and Factor 4, the component of spontaneous skin potential activity.

TABLE 4.6
VARIMAX FACTOR SCORES
INTRACLASS CORRELATIONS AND F-RATIOS

Factor	MZ		DZ		F
	n	r_I	n	r_I	
1	26	0·57‡	34	0·16	2·23†
2	26	0·66‡	34	0·64‡	1·52
3	26	0·60‡	34	0·46‡	1·50
4	26	0·54‡	34	0·10	2·60‡

† $p < 0.05$.
‡ $p < 0.01$.

The picture that emerges from this part of the analysis is a little simpler than that presented by the raw data discussed in the previous section. It seems possible to postulate four physiological systems: autonomic level (or balance), sympathetic responsivity, alpha activity, and spontaneous skin potential activity. The influence of heredity seems to be strongest in the case of the first and last of these, though it should be noted that none of the components accounts for all of the variance of the raw measures. Indeed, all four factors together accounted for less than half of the total variance. Even given a significant genetic component in certain aspects of the physiological processes examined here there is therefore still considerable scope for the influence of environmental factors, particularly on the raw measurements on which the analysis was based.

Further considerations

The data reported here were obtained as part of a larger study designed to investigate, at a physiological level, the concept of "arousal" (Hume, 1970). It is therefore of interest to consider the implications of t he present data within the wider context of that investigation. One purpose of the latter was to compare the correlations between the measures discussed above as they were found in groups of non-patients, neurotics, and psychotics; the general background being the earlier work of Claridge (1967) who had postulated that the relationship between different physiological systems may vary according to "nervous type". The results of that study, which underlined the variable nature of the correlations, were incorporated into a model proposing a construct of "input energy". This was assumed to determine the relationship between the various physiological systems, which were themselves defined in terms of the raw measures. It was argued that at low levels of input energy the physiological systems concerned varied independently of each other, beginning to covary at higher levels, at which point a small number of more complex dimensions appeared. At higher levels still it was suggested that dissociation takes place, with inhibitory systems becoming dominant.

One consequence of this model is that the analysis of large groups of subjects, comprising several smaller groups operating at different mean levels of "input energy", will result in the cancelling out of the different relationships obtaining within each subgroup. It seems reasonable to argue that this happened in the total twin group whose data were analysed here. Study of the relationships between the different physiological systems identified in certain subgroups of individuals might, therefore, be expected to reveal interesting results.

An immediate difficulty which arises, however, is the definition of subgroups. In Chapter 6 Dr Claridge, who undertakes a similar exercise, has chosen to use factor scores as his criteria and to compare the relationships between physiological measures and questionnaire responses. An alternative procedure, and the one used by Dr Claridge in his analysis of the sedation threshold data (Chapter 5), is to rely on a behavioural typology based on questionnaire scores, looking at the relationships between physiological measures in different personality, rather than "nervous", types. The latter method was chosen for analysing individual differences within our own data.

To this end the samples of 126 subjects for whom factor scores were available were classified according to their scores on the extraversion and neuroticism scales of the EPI, four groups being defined. These were "stable introverts", designated E−N−, "neurotic introverts" (E−N+), "stable extraverts" (E+N−), and "neurotic extraverts" (E+N+).

Cut-off points used to define these groups were scores of 14 and 11 on the E and N scales, respectively, both of these being as near to the median as possible.

The scores from the first four Varimax factors were then inter-correlated in each of these groups separately. The results are shown in Table 4.7, where it should be noted that the signs of the scores derived from Factor 3 have been reversed, so that an increase on all factors represents a decrease in physiological activity. Although the correlations shown in the table are small, a number of interesting trends are revealed. Comparing, first, "stable extraverts" and "stable introverts" (columns 1 and 3) it can be seen that at an equivalent, low, level of neuroticism, as one proceeds from extraversion to introversion there is a tendency for the correlations to increase, either becoming more positive, or changing from negative to positive. This trend is most marked in the case of the correlations between Factors 2 and 3 and between Factors 2 and 4, where the E—N— group showed values of +0·41 and +0·34, compared with those of —0·25 and —0·23 in the more extraverted group. In other words, at *low* levels of neuroticism, there is tendency for EEG activity, sympathetic responsiveness, and spontaneous skin potential activity to covary positively. A similar, though less marked, trend is found when the two extraverted groups, differing in neuroticism, are compared. Thus, looking at the correlations in columns 1 and 2 it can be seen that four out of the six values change from negative to positive with increasing neuroticism. This

TABLE 4.7
CORRELATIONS BETWEEN FACTOR SCORES FOR FOUR
QUESTIONNAIRE SUBGROUPS

Factors	E+N—	E+N+	E—N—	E—N+
1 and 2	—0·08	—0·05	+0·12	+0·05
1 and 3	—0·17	+0·12	+0·05	+0·11
1 and 4	—0·18	+0·03	—0·02	+0·11
2 and 3	—0·25	+0·15	+0·41	+0·11
2 and 4	—0·23	+0·15	+0·34	—0·23
3 and 4	+0·03	—0·23	+0·08	+0·13
N	31	31	25	39

tendency for neuroticism to be associated with a more uniform covariation of physiological activity is confined, however, to the extraverted half of the sample and does not appear in introverts, as can be seen by comparing the correlations in columns 3 and 4. Finally, it should be noted that we have considered only linear relationships between variables. However, although curvilinearity of regression cannot be ruled out, a superficial examination of the scatter plots for all of the scores suggested that in the present data such was not the case.

According to the model discussed earlier, increasing levels of "input energy" should be associated with increased covariation between physiological systems. The results just described would be consistent with that formulation since it is reasonable to argue that both introversion and neuroticism are characterized by heightened input energy. Certainly, evidence from work on the psychophysiological basis of those dimensions would support that view (Eysenck, 1967). It would be useful in this connection to try and find some parallel between our own findings and those reported by Dr Claridge elsewhere in the book, particularly those described by him in Chapter 6. Two problems make more than a superficial comparison difficult. First, as noted above the two studies used different methods of identifying "personality types". Secondly, the factors extracted by Dr Claridge from his principal components analysis of what was part of the present data—namely a smaller number of variables in those subjects who did the sedation threshold—were not identical to those described here; suggesting that his sample was not representative of the group as a whole. Nevertheless, some similarities between the two investigations can be observed. Both have emphasized the importance of EEG and autonomic factors as separate but interrelated physiological systems and both have provided evidence that it may be the covariation between such systems which is an important characteristic differentiating various personality types.

General conclusions

The results of our own twin study just described are generally consistent with the findings of previous investigations. Thus, there is some indication that certain single physiological measures, particularly of EEG and heart rate, together with some indices of sympathetic response, are influenced by genetic factors. Also confirmed is our conclusion from reviewing earlier evidence that it is valuable to examine composite, rather than single, physiological measures, a procedure little used in the past. Where this is done, as it was here, we have seen that it is possible to identify, by factor analysis, four major components which seem to represent meaningful physiological systems having varying degrees of genetic determination. Looked at from the point of view of their significance for behaviour, the importance of these components seems likely to be that of providing a biological basis for personality variation, their interaction apparently varying across individuals and according to the situation in which they are measured.

References

BARCAL, R., SIMON, J. and SOVA, J. (1969) Blood pressure in twins. *Lancet* **i**, 1321.

BLOCK, J. D. (1967) Monozygotic twin similarity in multiple psychophysiologic parameters and measures. *Recent Advances in Biological Psychiatry* **9**, 105–18.

BURCH, N. R. and GREINER, T. H. (1960) A bioelectric scale of human alertness. *Psychiat. res. Rep.* **12**, 183–93.

CATTELL, R. B. (1966) *Handbook of Multivariate Experimental Psychology*. Rand McNally, Chicago.

CHRISTIE, J. M. and VENABLES, P. H. (1971) Characteristics of palmar skin potential and conductance in relaxed human subjects. *Psychophysiology* **8**, 525–32.

CLARIDGE, G. S. (1967) *Personality and Arousal*. Pergamon, Oxford.

DOWNIE, W. W., BOYLE, J. A., GREIG, W. R., BUCHANAN, W. W. and ALEPA, F. P. (1969) Relative roles of genetic and environmental factors in control of blood pressure in normotensive subjects. *Brit. Heart J.* **31**, 21–25.

DUFFY, E. (1962) *Activation and Behaviour*. Wiley, New York.

DUSTMAN, R. E. and BECK, E. C. (1965) The visual evoked response in twins. *EEG clin. Neurophysiol.* **19**, 570–5.

EYSENCK, H. J. (1967) *The Biological Basis of Personality*. Charles C. Thomas, Springfield, Ill.

FREEMAN, G. L. and KATZOFF, E. T. (1942) Individual differences in physiological reactions to stimulation and their relation to other measures of emotionality. *J. exp. Psychol.* **31**, 527–37.

GELLHORN, E. (1967) *Principles of Autonomic-somatic Integrations*. Univ. Minnesota Press, Minneapolis.

GRAY, J. A. (1967) Strength of the nervous system, introversion–extraversion, conditionability, and arousal. *Behav. Res. Therap.* **5**, 151–69.

HOLLAND, H. C. (1965) *The Spiral After-effect*. Pergamon, Oxford.

HUME, W. I. (1966) Electrodermal measures in behavioural research. *J. psychosom. Res.* **9**, 383–91.

HUME, W. I. (1970) An experimental analysis of "arousal". Unpublished Ph.D. thesis, University of Bristol.

HUME, W. I. (1972a) Some physiological correlates of anxiety and extraversion. In press.

HUME, W. I. (1972b) The measurement of physiological arousal. In press.

HUME, W. I. and CLARIDGE, G. S. (1965) A comparison of two measures of "arousal" in normal subjects. *Life Sciences* **4**, 545–53.

JOST, H. and SONTAG, L. W. (1944) The genetic factor in autonomic nervous system function. *Psychosom. Med.* **6**, 308–10.

KRYSHOVA, N. A., BELIAEVA, Z. V., DMITRIEVA, A. F., ZHILINSKAIA, M. A. and PERVOV, L. G. (1962) Investigation of the higher nervous activity and of certain vegetative features in twins. *Soviet Psychol. and Psychiat.* **1**, 36–41.

LACEY, J. I. (1967) Somatic response patterning and stress: some revisions of activation theory. In Appley, M. H. and Trumbull, R. (Eds.) *Psychological Stress*. Appleton-Century-Crofts, New York.

LADER, M. H. and MONTAGU, J. D. (1962) The psychogalvanic reflex: a pharmacological study of the peripheral mechanism. *J. Neurol. Neurosurg. Psychiat.* **25**, 126–33.

LADER, M. H. and WING, L. (1966) *Physiological Measures, Sedative Drugs, and Morbid Anxiety*. Oxford Univ. Press, Oxford.

LANG, P. J. and HNATIOW, M. (1962) Stimulus repetition and the heart rate response. *J. comp. physiol. Psychol.* **55**, 781–5.

LINDSLEY, D. B. (1952) Psychological phenomena and the electroencephalogram. *EEG clin. Neurophysiol.* **4**, 443–56.

LYKKEN, D. T., ROSE, R., LUTHER, B. and MALEY, M. (1966) Correcting psychophysiological measures for individual differences in range. *Psychol. Bull.* **66**, 481–4.

MATHERS, J. A. L., OSBORNE, R. H. and DEGEORGE, F. V. (1961) Studies of blood pressure, heart rate and the electrocardiogram in adult twins. *Amer. Heart J.* **62**, 634–42.

MIALL, W. E., HENEAGE, P., KHOSIA, T., LOVELL, H. and MOORE, F. (1967) Factors influencing the degree of resemblance in arterial pressure in close relatives. *Clin. Sci.* **33**, 271–83.

MITTLER, P. (1971) *The Study of Twins*. Penguin, London.

MONTAGU, J. D. (1963) Habituation of the psychogalvanic reflex during serial tests. *J. psychosom. Res.*, **7**, 199–214.

OSBORNE, R. H., DEGEORGE, F. V. and MATHERS, J. A. L. (1963) The variability of blood pressure: basal and causal measurements in adult twins. *Amer. Heart J.* **66**, 176–83.

PAWLIK, K. and CATTELL, R. B. (1965) The relationship between certain personality factors and measures of cortical arousal. *Neuropsychologia* **3**, 129–51.

RACHMAN, S. (1960) Galvanic skin response in identical twins. *Psychol. Rep.* **6**, 298.

SHAPIRO, A. P., NICOTERO, J., SAPIRA, J. and SCHEIB, E. T. (1968) Analysis of the variability of blood pressure, pulse rate and catecholamine responsivity in identical and fraternal twins. *Psychosom. Med.* **30**, 506–20.

SHEPHERD, J. T. (1963) *Physiology of the Circulation in Human Limbs in Health and Disease*. Saunders, Philadelphia.

STOCKS, P. (1930) A biometric investigation of twins and their brothers and sisters. *Ann. Eugen.* **4**, 49–108.

VANDENBERG, S. G., CLARK, P. J. and SAMUELS, I. (1965) Psychophysiological reactions of twins: hereditary factors in galvanic skin resistance, heart beat, and breathing rates. *Eugen. Quart.* **12,** 7–10.

VENABLES, P. H. and SAYER, E. (1963) On the measurement of the level of skin potential. *Brit. J. Psychol.* **54,** 251–60.

WENGER, M. A. (1948) Studies of autonomic balance in Army, Air Force personnel. *Comp. Psychol. Monogr.* **19,** 1–111.

WENGER, M. A. (1962) Some problems in psychophysiological research.   In Roessler, R. and Greenfield, N. S. (Eds.) *Physiological Correlates of Psychological Disorder.* University of Wisconsin, Madison.

WENGER, M. A. and ELLINGTON, M. (1943) The measurement of autonomic balance in children: method and normative data. *Psychosom. Med.* **5,** 241–53.

YOUNG, J. P. R. and FENTON, G. W. (1971) An investigation of the genetic aspects of the alpha attenuation response. *Psychol. Med.* **1,** 365–71.

ZWEIFLER, A. J., CUSHING, G. and CONWAY, J. (1967) The relationship between pulse volume and blood flow in the finger. *Angiology* **18,** 591–7.

CHAPTER 5

SEDATIVE DRUG TOLERANCE
IN TWINS

By GORDON CLARIDGE and ESTHER ROSS

Introduction

From Pavlov onwards, workers adopting a nervous typological approach to individual differences have been interested in the use of drug techniques as experimental tools for exploring the psychophysiological correlates of personality. The logic of using drugs for this purpose is straightforward. It is assumed that drugs acting on the central nervous system do so by affecting the very same mechanisms or processes that form the psychophysiological basis of personality. A given drug should therefore have a different effect or produce a different degree of change depending on the individual's nervous, and hence personality, type. One research strategy for investigating the problem is the determination of individual variations in the tolerance of centrally acting drugs. This involves simply measuring the amount of drug required to bring about a predetermined change in the individual's behaviour or physiological state. The quantity of drug administered up to that point then provides an index of his tolerance for it. For obvious reasons the depressant, rather than the stimulant, drugs have been more often chosen for study in this way, the most widely used procedure being the estimation of tolerance for one of the barbiturates. This "sedation threshold" technique, as it is called, was first described by Shagass (1954) and in its original form involved determining from changes in the frontal EEG an individual's tolerance of intravenous amylobarbitone sodium. Subsequent modifications to the technique have included the use of other barbiturates, particularly thiopentone,

115

and the adoption of other criteria, either physiological (Perez-Reyes *et al.*, 1962) or behavioural (Claridge and Herrington, 1960), for assessing the threshold of sedation.

Studies using these different methods of determining the sedation threshold have consistently shown that individual differences in the tolerance of barbiturates are related to personality, though most of the work to date has been done with psychiatric patients. The relevant evidence has been reviewed elsewhere (Claridge, 1967, 1970), but may be summarized as follows. In populations of neurotics, variations in sedative drug tolerance are known to parallel a broad personality dimension of dysthymia-(or obsessionality) hysteria. High sedation thresholds, i.e. high tolerance of barbiturates, have been shown to characterize those obsessional, anxious neurotics at the dysthymic end of the continuum; while low tolerance is more often associated with hysterical and psychopathic syndromes. These results are in keeping with other findings demonstrating that neurotics at opposite ends of the dysthymia-hysteria continuum differ in central nervous arousability. Thus, dysthymics, in addition to their strong tolerance of sedatives, physiologically show a marked sympathetic reaction to stress and perform at a high level of efficiency on tasks of sustained attention, such as vigilance. Hysterico-psychopaths, on the other hand, in keeping with their poor resistance to the effects of barbiturates, show evidence of low physiological and psychological arousal. Such findings are therefore consistent with the nervous typological model of personality.

Comparatively little work has been done with sedation threshold procedures in non-hospitalized normal subjects. Therefore less is known about the correlation between drug tolerance and personality analysed in terms of normal personality dimensions and traits, as distinct from characteristics derived from the description of psychiatric patients. This is not to say that no attention has been paid to the problem. Eysenck (1957), in the statement of his original theory of personality, incorporated an explicit postulate linking introversion–extraversion to individual differences in drug response. With respect to sedatives he hypothesized that introverts should have greater tolerance of these drugs than extraverts. The evidence that has accumulated since then has suggested, however, that the relationships between drug response and personality are more complex than that, a fact recently admitted by Eysenck (1967) in the revision of his theory. The consensus of opinion would now seem to be that at the very least both of the dimensions emphasized by Eysenck, extraversion and neuroticism, are probably implicated. Thus, in an early study of the sedation threshold Shagass and Jones (1958) concluded that variations on the test were related to introversion and manifest anxiety—an equivalent of neuroticism—both operating to increase barbiturate tolerance. Claridge and Herrington (1960) also reported that introversion was significantly and positively correlated with sedation threshold in a small group of normal subjects, but when the sample was increased in size the correlation fell to zero (Claridge, 1967). In that extended sample there was a significant relationship with neuroticism, though *negative* in direction, indicating that the more neurotic subjects had lower depressant drug tolerance. Rodnight and Gooch (1963), using a nitrous oxide gas technique, rather than the conventional sedation threshold procedure, clarified the picture a little by showing in a group of normal subjects that tolerance for that drug was determined by a complex interaction between extraversion and neuroticism. Thus, whether extraversion correlated positively or negatively with tolerance depended on the degree of neuroticism present. Similarly, the correlation between drug tolerance and neuroticism was opposite in direction in introverts and extraverts.

One purpose of the present study was to extend to normal subjects our previous work on the sedation threshold in psychiatric patients and examine in more detail some of the relationships which it appeared might exist between descriptive personality characteristics and the tolerance of barbiturates, in this case amylobarbitone sodium. The account of this aspect of the results given here will be confined to a simple analysis of the relationship between the drug tolerance test used —the sedation threshold—and scores derived from personality questionnaires. However, in the next chapter we shall return to the data and consider some of their implications viewed within the broader context of nervous typological theory.

A second, and of course equally important, aim of this study of sedation threshold in twins was to examine the extent to which genetic factors contribute to individual differences in the tolerance of barbiturates. It was considered that, even if drug tolerance proved to be unrelated to personality, the study would in itself be a useful exercise in pharmacogenetics since, as far as we know, the sedation threshold has never previously been investigated from this point of view. Indeed, the whole problem of the role of genetic factors in determining the behavioural, as distinct from the biochemical, response to drugs is virtually unexplored. Two previous studies which are vaguely relevant to that described here were both concerned with caffeine, though neither involved a systematic comparison of MZ and DZ samples. In an early study of a single MZ pair, Glass (1954) showed a remarkable similarity in the performance curves of the two twins working on a target aiming task after a small dose of caffeine. More recently Abe (1968), investigating a group of 11 MZ twins, reported that the pair members were significantly alike in some of their subjective psychological reactions to caffeine. Prior to the present study there was therefore some, rather limited, evidence that MZ and DZ twins might differ in the extent to which they resembled each other in their behavioural response to centrally acting drugs.

Selection of subjects

Compared with the main project, the sample of twins it was possible to obtain for this part of the investigation was relatively small. There were three reasons for this. First, determination of the sedation threshold necessitated a return visit to our department, again involving a whole day. Secondly, only a limited number of the subjects approached were, understandably, willing to submit to the intravenous injection required by the sedation threshold technique. Thirdly, in the interests of safety it was essential to adhere to strict criteria of suitability for administration of the test. These were achieved by screening potential subjects in three stages. In the first place an upper age limit of forty years was imposed, all twins younger than this being approached and asked if they were willing to volunteer for the sedation threshold procedure, which was explained fully to them. Twins who volunteered were then questioned closely about their health, particularly with respect to any physical condition which would contraindicate the administration of an intravenous barbiturate. Finally, on the day of the test they were physically examined and, as a double check, questioned again about their health record.

The final sample obtained in this way consisted of eleven pairs of MZ and ten pairs of DZ twins. Despite the age criterion applied, most of the twins were actually well below forty years, the bias towards youth being particularly evident in the MZ sample. The mean age for the latter was 19·19, SD 1·47 years, while the mean for DZ twins was 24·30, SD 7·12 years. The difference in age between the two samples, although relatively small, unfortunately proved to be significant, t being 2·34 ($p < 0.05$, d.f. 19). However, as will be discussed later, this is unlikely to have had any material influence on the comparison of sedation threshold in the MZ and DZ groups.

Quite clearly the twin sample used for the sedation threshold study was not an ideal one and for this reason the conclusions to be drawn from the results to be reported are inevitably somewhat limited. The difficulties of obtaining representative samples of twins have already been referred to in an earlier chapter. In the present instance the problem was further aggravated by the need to impose the strict standards of acceptability described above for participation in this part of the project. However, it goes without saying that in this respect we considered it vital to err on the side of caution.

Sedation threshold procedure

In each set of twins the sedation threshold was performed on both members of the pair on the same day, and always in the morning. For one half of the sample the younger member was tested first, followed immediately by his or her twin. In the other half of the sample this order was reversed. The twins were instructed to come to the department having had no more than a light breakfast consisting of a cup of tea or coffee and two slices of buttered toast. After the arrival of the pair they were physically examined and their weights, in light indoor clothes, recorded to the nearest kilogramme.

The sedation thresholds were then determined using the method originally described by Claridge and Herrington (op. cit.). This involves presenting to the subject a tape-recorded series of random digits played at the rate of one digit every 2 sec. The subject is required to respond by doubling the digits while receiving a continuous intravenous infusion of amylobarbitone sodium, prepared in a solution of 1 g in 20 ml of water and administered at a constant rate of 2 ml/min. The injection is continued until response errors or failures to respond exceed 50% in two consecutive blocks of five digits. The amount of drug administered up to that point is then recorded and divided by the subject's weight to give a measure of the sedation threshold in mg/kg. At the end of the test the twins were allowed to recover and then driven home with instructions not to drink alcohol or take other sedative drugs for a period of at least 24 hr.

Although the experimental procedure outlined above was followed exactly in the present study it is necessary to comment briefly on our use of body weight in the calculation of the sedation threshold. While it is conventional pharmacological practice to apply such a correction, a recent study by one of us (Claridge, 1971) demonstrated over several groups of subjects that the procedure has little rationale, at least in the case of intravenously administered amylobarbitone sodium. Thus, it was found that the correlations between weight and uncorrected drug dosage required to reach threshold ranged in different samples from zero to very slightly positive, weight over the total group taking up only about 3% of the variance. However, because weight does appear to exert some influence, if only at the extremes, we decided to continue correcting for it in the present study. In practice the results are unlikely to be affected either way since in the investigation just quoted it was shown that there was an extremely high correlation ($+0.96$) between uncorrected and weight-corrected drug dosage required to reach threshold.

Comparison of MZ and DZ twins

Considering, first, the absolute sedation threshold values across the total twin sample, that is MZ and DZ combined, the mean for all forty-two individuals was 8·13, SD 2·18 mg/kg. For the MZ twins ($N = 22$) the mean was 7·43, SD 2·08 mg/kg and for the DZ twins ($N = 20$) it was 8·91, SD 2·46 mg/kg. DZ pairs, therefore, had a somewhat higher average threshold and a slightly greater range, but for the group as a whole both the mean and standard deviation were comparable to those found in other normal subjects tested with the same procedure (Claridge,

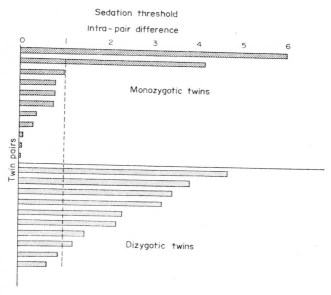

FIG. 5.1. Diagram showing the intra-pair difference score on sedation threshold for each set of monozygotic and dizygotic twins.

1967). In terms of sedation threshold, therefore, the present sample was not particularly unusual.

Turning to the relative similarity of MZ and DZ twins on the test, these data are presented in Fig. 5.1 as intra-pair difference scores for each individual set of twins. The mean intra-pair difference score for MZ twins was 0·84 mg/kg and for DZ twins 2·42 mg/kg. The *average* difference between DZ pairs was therefore almost three times that of MZ pairs. However, inspection of Fig. 5.1 illustrates how there was a marked difference in the distribution of scores in the two samples. The most striking fact was the very large difference in sedation threshold found in two of the MZ pairs. The other nine pairs who were similar were remarkably so, two actually having almost identical sedation thresholds. The DZ group, by comparison, showed a much more even distribution of difference scores.

The unusual distribution found in the MZ group posed a problem concerning the appropriate statistical technique with which to compare the two twin samples. The inevitably large variance of the MZ group meant that it did not differ significantly from the DZ group when tested with intraclass correlations or an F-ratio for within-pair variance comparison. This lack of significance nevertheless clearly masked a difference between the samples, evident on visual inspection of the data. It was therefore decided to test statistical significance by comparing the frequency with which pairs in each group differed in sedation threshold by more than or less than 1 mg/kg. It was considered that this was a relatively rigorous cut-off point, bearing in mind that the absolute sedation thresholds averaged about 8 mg/kg. Put another way, a difference of 1 mg/kg represents for a person of average weight only 70 mg of amylobarbitone sodium.

Divided according to this criterion the relative frequencies shown in Fig. 5.2 were obtained. It can be seen that nine out of the eleven MZ pairs had sedation thresholds which differed by 1 mg/kg or less; whereas eight out of ten DZ twins differed by more than that amount. Tested with the Fisher exact probability test it was found that these two distributions differed significantly at the 0·01 level. As a group trend, therefore, there was evidence that MZ twins are significantly more alike in sedation threshold than DZ twins.

However, because of the fact that the two groups differed in age it is necessary to consider whether the greater similarity of MZ twins was due to their being on average a younger sample of individuals. This possibility was tested out by correlating age with the sedation threshold intra-pair difference scores in the DZ twins only, a similar calculation not being carried out in the MZ sample because the very restricted age range in that group would have considerably attenuated any correlation that existed. The value for *rho* in the DZ group proved to be +0·30. This figure was not significant and, while the direction of the correlation does suggest a slight tendency for older twins to show a greater difference in sedation threshold, the association clearly cannot account entirely for the closer similarity of MZ twins on the test.

There remains, of course, the problem of explaining the very marked discordance found in two of the MZ pairs. One possible explanation is that the pairs in question were not monozygotic at all. However, this

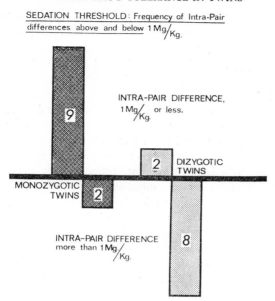

SEDATION THRESHOLD: Frequency of Intra-Pair differences above and below 1 Mg/Kg.

INTRA-PAIR DIFFERENCE, 1 Mg/Kg. or less.

9

2

DIZYGOTIC TWINS

MONOZYGOTIC TWINS

2

INTRA-PAIR DIFFERENCE more than 1 Mg/Kg.

8

FIG. 5.2. Diagram showing the number of monozygotic and dizygotic twins whose sedation thresholds differed by more than and less than 1 mg/kg.

is unlikely because, as described in Chapter 1, the methods used for determining zygosity were extremely thorough, leading to low average odds on misclassification. Furthermore, the actual odds on zygosity in the two discrepant pairs were double-checked following the discovery of their sedation threshold differences. Another possibility is that there had been a technical error in determining the sedation threshold for one member of each pair. This was ruled out in the case of one of the pairs—those with the greater difference in sedation threshold—by repeating the test on both twins. The intra-pair difference on this second occasion proved to be even greater—8·1 mg/kg as against 6·1 mg/kg for the first testing.

A more likely explanation is that some environmental factor operated to make the discordant twins less alike in drug tolerance, though the differences observed appeared to be specific to the sedation threshold. Thus, an intensive search through the other data we had collected in the course of the twin study revealed that in the case of neither pair were there any obvious differences in cognitive function, personality, or physiological response. In the case of one of the pairs, therefore, no explanation can be offered for their discordance in sedation threshold.

However, in the second pair of twins—those on whom the test had been repeated—some clues did emerge which made it possible to speculate, at least, on some possible reasons for their discordance. It was discovered that one member of the pair—the twin with the higher sedation threshold—suffered from congenital talipes (clubfoot). Clubfoot is thought to be mainly due to mechanical pressure inside the womb, though it is interesting that, reflecting the generally greater susceptibility of MZ twins to congenital abnormalities, it occurs more frequently in monozygotic than in dizygotic twinning (Carter, 1965). While it seems unlikely that the observed difference in drug tolerance could be specifically related, in an aetiological sense, to the presence of clubfoot in one of the twins, it is possible that it resulted from a generally more abnormal intra-uterine environment in the pair in question. Certainly when we looked into the birth history of the pair it emerged that the pregnancy had been very abnormal and the birth extremely difficult. It is just feasible that their pre-natal environment had been sufficiently pathological to cause, apart from the clubfoot, other physiological differences, perhaps involving the central nervous system and hence the response to psychotropic drugs.

Another explanation for the results in this pair was offered by Mr Blockley, surgeon in charge of the Orthopaedic Department at the Royal Hospital for Sick Children in Glasgow whose advice was sought about the problem. He suggested that since it was the twin with talipes who had the higher sedation threshold the reason may lie in her increased resistance to barbiturates due to previously repeated administration of sedation and anaesthetics required for operative correction of the disability. The main objection to this explanation is that the evidence, reviewed elsewhere by Herrington (1967), would suggest that such acquired tolerance is unlikely to have much effect on the dose of drug required to induce sedation but is more likely to be reflected in the rate of recovery from anaesthetics; in other words, in the "sleeping time". This view would tend to be supported by clinical observations made during this and other studies of the sedation threshold and suggesting that, among those given similar amounts of barbiturate, the people who recover rapidly from the procedure are frequently individuals in whom there is evidence of previous habitual exposure to other depressants, such as alcohol.

Whatever the true reason for the discordance in sedation threshold observed in the two MZ pairs just described, the results as a whole clearly illustrate the powerful effects of both environmental and hereditary factors on barbiturate tolerance. As a statistical trend the evidence points to a significant genetic determination of the characteristic. At the same time its phenotypic expression in the individual case is obviously capable of being modified to a marked degree by non-genetic influences.

Personality correlates of sedation threshold

The relationships between barbiturate tolerance and personality were examined by correlating the sedation threshold with scores derived from some of the questionnaires administered previously to the twins and described by Mrs Canter in Chapter 2. Three questionnaires were chosen for investigation, namely the Eysenck Personality Inventory (EPI), Cattell's 16PF, and the Sociability/Impulsivity Scale. These were selected because they all yielded measures of personality characteristics related to the two major dimensions which were of greatest theoretical interest, namely introversion–extraversion and anxiety/neuroticism. For the purpose of the present analysis, in order to provide more reliable measures of these dimensions, the equivalent scores from the EPI and 16PF were combined. That is to say, a composite extraversion score was obtained from the appropriate EPI scale and its 16PF second-order factor equivalent. Similarly, an anxiety/neuroticism score was calculated by combining the EPI N-scale with the 16PF second-order factor of Anxiety with which the former is highly correlated. For computational purposes the appropriate measures from the two questionnaires were averaged, those derived from the EPI scales being converted to sten scores, the 16PF factor scores already being in that form. The four personality dimensions investigated therefore were Anxiety/neuroticism (called here N), Extraversion (E), Sociability, and Impulsivity.

For the total group of forty-two subjects available, product moment correlations were first calculated between sedation threshold and each of these four personality measures. All of the correlations proved to be very low, none even approaching an acceptable level of significance. Considering extraversion first, E itself correlated only -0.15, while for its two components, Sociability and Impulsivity, the values for r were even lower, being -0.04 and -0.10, respectively. The correlation between anxiety/neuroticism and sedation threshold was only slightly higher, r being $+0.26$.

This lack of association between barbiturate tolerance and anxiety/ neuroticism and extraversion, considered as independent dimensions was not, of course, unexpected. As pointed out earlier, previous evidence would suggest that the personality determination of drug response involves a more complex interaction between E and N, a possibility that was tested here by carrying out what Eysenck (1967) has termed "zone analysis". The method entails comparing the performance of individuals showing each of the four combinations of E and N according to the zone or quadrant they occupy in the two-dimensional space formed by introversion–extraversion and anxiety/neuroticism. Using this procedure it is possible to determine whether anxiety/neuroticism, for example, has a different relationship with some experimental variable in introverts compared with extraverts. Looked at the other way round, the influence of extraversion can be compared in people high and low on the anxiety/neuroticism dimension.

One way of carrying out zone analysis, and that adopted here, is to select two groups of high and low N subjects and then compute separate correlations between extraversion and the experimental variable under investigation, in this case sedation threshold. The analysis is completed by dividing the sample into high and low E scorers and correlating anxiety/neuroticism with the variable in each of these two groups.

For present purposes high and low scorers were defined as subjects falling, respectively, in the upper and lower thirds of the distribution on each of the two main dimensions, E and N. Since there was a total sample of forty-two subjects available this meant that there were fourteen individuals in each of the four possible groups of High N, Low N, High E, and Low E. Dividing the group in this way resulted in the High N sample being comprised of individuals with sten scores of 7 or more. The lower cut-off point on that dimension was 5·3, though eleven out of the fourteen Low N subjects had sten scores below five. For the High and Low E groups the cut-off points were sten scores of 6·5 or above and 4·5 or below, respectively.

Considering, first, the division of the sample according to extraversion, it was found that the correlation between anxiety/neuroticism and sedation threshold was opposite in sign in introverts and extraverts. In High E subjects the value for *rho* was −0·65 ($p < 0.02$), indicating that among extraverts increasing anxiety/neuroticism leads to a lower sedation threshold. The equivalent correlation in Low E subjects was +0·34, a value which was not significant but which suggests some tendency for barbiturate tolerance to be greater as anxiety/neuroticism increases in introverts.

When the data were considered according to the division in terms of anxiety/neuroticism a similar reversal of correlation was found. In High N subjects *rho* between extraversion and sedation threshold was −0·45, a value just missing significance at the 0·05 level. In Low N subjects, on the other hand, the correlation was significant and positive, *rho* being +0·65 ($p < 0.05$). In other words, among individuals with high levels of anxiety/neuroticism it is the introverts who have the greater tolerance of barbiturates; in those with *low* anxiety/neuroticism extraverts have the greater tolerance.

In view of these findings it was further decided to examine how the two components of extraversion contributed to the interacting influence of E and N on sedation threshold. Correlations were therefore calculated between sedation threshold and both Sociability and Impulsivity scores in the High and Low N groups. Taking High N subjects first, it was found that in these individuals threshold correlated −0·59 ($p < 0.05$) with Impulsivity and −0·14 (NS) with Sociability. In Low N subjects the correlations were +0·31 (NS) and +0·61 ($p < 0.05$), respectively. Thus, as expected the pattern of association for the two components taken separately was similar to that found for extraversion as a more general dimension. However, the relative influence of sociability and impulsivity differed in High and Low N individuals. In the former impulsivity seemed to be the more important component, greater impulsiveness leading to lower tolerance. In subjects with low anxiety/neuroticism, however, sociability made a more significant contribution, more sociable individuals having higher thresholds.

To summarize, then, it would appear that the response to barbiturates is not related to extraversion or anxiety/neuroticism *per se* but to combinations of personality characteristics that reflect the interaction between both of these dimensions. It is interesting to note, in this respect, that the pattern of correlations found here is exactly the same as that reported by Rodnight and Gooch (op. cit.) in their similar study of nitrous oxide. It would seem that high sedative drug tolerance is characteristic of more neurotic, self-controlled introverts, on the one hand, and sociable, unanxious extraverts, on the other. Poor tolerance is found significantly more often in impulsive, neurotic extraverts and in withdrawn introverts who lack anxiety. These results therefore help to clarify even further some of the relationships which have been felt to exist between personality factors and individual differences in the response to drugs.

Discussion and conclusions

As discussed at the beginning of this chapter, the purpose of carrying out the study reported here was twofold: first, to examine the genetic contribution to individual differences in barbiturate tolerance and, secondly, to use the sedation threshold as a technique for exploring the nervous typological basis of personality. On both counts the investigation can be said to have yielded encouraging results. Looked at from a genetic viewpoint the data have provided evidence that the tolerance of barbiturates is determined to a significant degree by heredity though, like all behavioural characteristics, it is capable of being modified by environmental influences occurring during the life-history of the individual. As far as the relationships between personality and sedation threshold are concerned, the results indicate an interacting influence of both extraversion and anxiety/neuroticism on barbiturate tolerance. Although the theoretical evaluation of these findings will be undertaken in the following chapter, some comments of a more general nature are appropriate here.

The results can be most logically discussed in terms of the differences found here between individuals high in anxiety/neuroticism and those low on that dimension. In the former group the tendency for introverts to have high, and extraverts to have low, barbiturate tolerance is entirely consistent with previous studies of the sedation threshold in psychiatric patients who, because of their diagnosis, can also be assumed to have high anxiety/neuroticism. Thus, there is good evidence that neurotics of the introverted type, such as obsessionals and other dysthymics, have significantly greater barbiturate tolerance than those showing the hysterical or psychopathic disorders of the extravert (Shagass and Jones, op. cit.; Shagass and Kerenyi, 1958; Claridge, 1967). Indeed, it is of interest to note that Eysenck's original predictions concerning drug response differences in introverts and extraverts are in fact supported when applied to individuals falling at the high end of the anxiety/neuroticism dimension.

Eysenck's model clearly cannot account for the reversal of relationship found between sedation threshold and introversion–extraversion in individuals with *low* anxiety/neuroticism. However, one possibility and one for which there is some experimental support is that low levels on that dimension actually represent a form of *psychoticism*. Eysenck has always regarded the latter as a third, independent, personality dimension which he has recently attempted to measure with the P (psychoticism) scale of his new PEN questionnaire (Eysenck and Eysenck, 1968). However, there is some reason to believe that the scale taps only psychotic characteristics of a particular kind, namely those of a paranoid nature, and fails to measure such features of psychosis as blunting of effect and lack of drive. It has been argued elsewhere (Claridge and Chappa, to appear) that these characteristics may be reflected in low levels of reported neuroticism and that low N scoring and high P scoring may represent different aspects of a common psychoticism dimension. In support of their thesis Claridge and Chappa reported the results of a psychophysiological study of normal subjects classified into High P, High N, and Low N individuals according to their scores on Eysenck's PEN questionnaire. The method of psychophysiological analysis they adopted was derived from previous research on psychotic patients, in whom it has been found that the correlations between measures of "autonomic" and "cortical" arousal are opposite in sign to those observed in non-psychotic individuals (Venables, 1963; Lykken and Maley, 1968; Herrington and Claridge, 1965). Using the two-flash threshold and skin conductance as their psychophysiological indices, Claridge and Chappa found that the relationship between the two measures was identical in High P and Low N individuals and opposite in direction to that seen in High N subjects. These results were interpreted as evidence that Low N and High P individuals share a particular kind of nervous typological organization similar to that found in clinical psychosis.

Returning to the positive correlation found here between sedation threshold and extraversion in Low N subjects, how far is that result consistent with the interpretation that low anxiety/neuroticism represents part of a general personality dimension of psychoticism? The crucial data should come from correlating extraversion with sedation threshold in psychotic patients. To the writers' knowledge only one such study has been carried out (Claridge, 1967). He did find the expected tendency for extraverted psychotics to have higher sedation thresholds than introverted psychotics, though the correlation, obtained on a small sample of fifteen patients, was not significant, r being $+0.32$. However, it is perhaps worth pointing out that this result is in keeping with clinical evidence from the same study suggesting that, among psychotics, it is the more socially and emotionally active who tend to have the greater barbiturate tolerance. Indeed, it was on the basis of findings of this kind that led Claridge to propose his model of personality which would predict positive relationships between extraversion and sedation threshold in certain normal individuals. This model will be discussed in more detail in the following chapter. However, in the meantime and in the narrower context of the study reported here, it seems possible to reach two conclusions. The first is that personality characteristics have a significant influence on the tolerance of barbiturates in normal subjects. The second is that in so far as the sedation threshold represents part of the nervous typological basis of these characteristics personality at that level can be said to be determined to a significant degree by genetic factors.

References

ABE, K. (1968) Reactions to coffee and alcohol in monozygotic twins. *J. psychosom. Res.* **12,** 199–203.

CARTER, C. O. (1965) The inheritance of common congenital malformations. *Prog. med. Genet.* **4,** 59–84.

CLARIDGE, G. S. (1967) *Personality and Arousal*. Pergamon, Oxford.

CLARIDGE, G. S. (1970) *Drugs and Human Behaviour*. Allen Lane the Penguin Press, London.

CLARIDGE, G. S. (1971) The relative influence of weight and of "nervous type" on the tolerance of amylobarbitone sodium. *Brit. J. Anaesth.* **43**, 1121–5.

CLARIDGE, G. S. and CHAPPA, H. J. (to appear) Psychoticism: a study of its biological basis in normal subjects. *Brit. J. soc. clin. Psychol.*

CLARIDGE, G. S. and HERRINGTON, R. N. (1960) Sedation threshold, personality and the theory of neurosis. *J. ment. Sci.* **106**, 1568–83.

EYSENCK, H. J. (1957) Drugs and personality. I. Theory and methodology. *J. ment. Sci.* **103**, 119–31.

EYSENCK, H. J. (1967) *The Biological Basis of Personality*. Charles C. Thomas, Springfield, Ill.

EYSENCK, H. J. and EYSENCK, S. B. G. (1968) The measurement of psychoticism: a study of factor stability and reliability. *Brit. J. soc. clin. Psychol.* **7**, 286–94.

GLASS, H. B. (1954) Genetic aspects of adaptability. In *Genetics and the Inheritance of Integrated Neurological and Psychiatric Patterns. Proceedings of Research in Nervous and Mental Disease*, vol. 33. Williams and Wilkins, Baltimore.

HERRINGTON, R. N. (1967) The sedation threshold: pharmacological considerations. In Claridge, G. S. *Personality and Arousal*. Pergamon, Oxford.

HERRINGTON, R. N. and CLARIDGE, G. S. (1965) Sedation threshold and Archimedes spiral after-effect in early psychosis. *J. psychiat. Res.* **3**, 159–70.

LYKKEN, D. T. and MALEY, M. (1968) Autonomic versus cortical arousal in schizophrenics and non-psychotics. *J. psychiat. Res.* **6**, 21–32.

PEREZ-REYES, M., SHANDS, H. C. and JOHNSON, G. (1962) Galvanic skin reflex inhibition threshold: a new psychophysiologic technique. *Psychosom. Med.* **24**, 274–7.

RODNIGHT, E. and GOOCH, R. N. (1963) A new method for the determination of individual differences in susceptibility to a depressant drug. In Eysenck, H. J. (Ed.) *Experiments with Drugs*. Pergamon, Oxford.

SHAGASS, C. (1954) The sedation threshold. A method for estimating tension in psychiatric patients. *EEG clin. Neurophysiol.* **6**, 221–33.

SHAGASS, C. and JONES, A. L. (1958) A neurophysiological test for psychiatric diagnosis: results in 750 patients. *Amer. J. Psychiat.* **114**, 1002–9.

SHAGASS, C. and KERENYI, A. B. (1958) Neurophysiologic studies of personality. *J. nerv. ment. Dis.* **126**, 141–7.

VENABLES, P. H. (1963) The relationship between level of skin potential and fusion of paired light flashes in schizophrenic and normal subjects. *J. psychiat. Res.* **1**, 279–87.

CHAPTER 6

A NERVOUS TYPOLOGICAL ANALYSIS OF PERSONALITY VARIATION IN NORMAL TWINS

By GORDON CLARIDGE

A model of personality

As the previous chapters of this book have demonstrated, a very large quantity of information covering a wide range of behaviour was accumulated on our twin sample. So far the data have been looked at mainly from a genetic viewpoint, each measure being considered separately or as part of a set of variables tapping similar areas of psychological or physiological response. The purpose of the present chapter is to change this emphasis somewhat and to attempt an integration of certain parts of the data by examining the interrelationships between different kinds of measure. In doing so we shall be guided by the nervous typological theory of individual differences within which the project was planned and in particular by the model of personality earlier proposed by Claridge (1967). As discussed in Chapter 1, this approach, in which a defined theoretical viewpoint could be tested out by examining appropriate relationships within the data, was considered preferable to the less systematic alternative, namely that of factor analysing all of the measures obtained in the research and hoping for psychological meaning to emerge. In any case, quite apart from the methodological advantages of adopting this theory-directed approach, the availability of relevant data on a group of mentally well subjects provided an ideal opportunity for testing the present author's model, which was derived largely from studies of psychiatric patients.

132

The model, together with the extensive experimental evidence on which it was based, have been fully discussed elsewhere and for more complete details the reader is referred to the original monograph (Claridge, op. cit.). However, the essential features of the theory proposed there are illustrated in Fig. 6.1. As a nervous typological

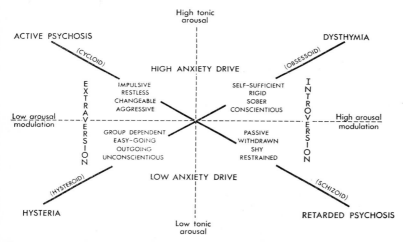

FIG. 6.1. Diagram illustrating the author's descriptive model of personality. Broken lines refer to two underlying causal mechanisms (see text) determining two behavioural continua of neuroticism and psychoticism, represented by solid lines. Also shown are some of the descriptive features of normal personality expected in individuals falling in various positions along the two continua. (Taken from Claridge, G. S. (1967) *Personality and Arousal*. Pergamon, Oxford.)

model the theory proposes certain relationships between descriptive personality characteristics and underlying psychophysiological parameters. At the descriptive level two major personality dimensions are recognized, namely neuroticism and psychoticism, the end-points of each being defined by appropriate forms of neurosis and psychosis. Thus, neuroticism is seen as a continuum running from dysthymia to hysteria, while emotionally active and withdrawn or retarded psychotics, respectively, define the opposite poles of psychoticism. Since neuroticism and psychoticism are regarded as continuously variable dimensions running through the general population they are also assumed to account for normal personality differences, particularly those related to extraversion and its component traits. Some of the characteristics tentatively thought to be associated with relative loadings on neuroticism and psychoticism are shown in Fig. 6.1.

At the psychophysiological, or nervous typological, level the main difference between neuroticism and psychoticism is assumed to lie in the manner in which two important causal processes interact or co-vary. These two processes, isolated by statistical analysis of psychophysiological data, have been named *tonic arousal* and *arousal modulation*. The former refers to arousal as conventionally defined by activation theorists and appears to have its major loadings on measures of autonomic reactivity and, of interest in the present context, the sedation threshold. Arousal modulation is a more difficult concept but statistically is mainly associated with EEG parameters, such as alpha index and alpha frequency; though in the original study it also seemed to be reflected in such perceptual phenomena as the spiral after-effect. Arousal modulation is regarded as having a CNS regulating function and to be concerned with the monitoring of sensory input and with such processes as narrowing and broadening of attention. The general manner in which these two mechanisms are thought to be functionally related is illustrated diagrammatically in Fig. 6.2.

The way in which tonic arousal and arousal modulation are considered to provide a nervous typological basis for neuroticism and psychoticism can be seen by referring back to Fig. 6.1. Essentially the model proposes that the two psychophysiological mechanisms covary in opposite directions along the two dimensions. In the case of neuroticism they are related in such a way that, for example, individuals in the dysthymic or obsessoid quadrant show a high level of tonic arousal but an equally high degree of arousal modulation. Individuals in the hysteroid quadrant, on the other hand, show appropriately low levels of activity in both systems. In both cases tonic arousal and arousal modulation are matched in strength. Psychoticism, however, represents a state of affairs in which the two hypothetical processes covary in a relatively "dissociated" fashion, dissociated that is with respect to neuroticism. As with the latter, the *level* of tonic arousal (and arousal modulation) will differ according to the individual's position along the psychoticism dimension, but in this case the two processes will vary in

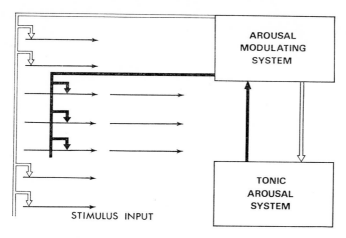

Fig. 6.2. Schematic diagram illustrating the author's causal model of nervous typological organization. Thick black arrows represent activating or facilitating influences and white arrows inhibitory influences. The arousal modulating system is assumed to exert an inhibitory control over the tonic arousal system as well as to filter, by inhibition and facilitation, the sensory input into both systems. Differences in the balance between the two systems are considered to account for nervous typological, and hence personality, variations (see text). (Taken from Claridge, G. S. (1967) *Personality and Arousal*. Pergamon, Oxford.)

opposite directions with respect to each other. Thus, those people in the cycloid quadrant shown in Fig. 6.1 will resemble dysthymics in having a high level of tonic arousal but, unlike them, will show *weak* modulation of sensory input. Conversely, individuals in the schizoid quadrant will show low tonic arousal and high arousal modulation.

The model just described was partly developed out of that proposed by Eysenck (1957) and before considering its application to the present data it may be useful to clarify some of the points of departure between the two theories. They in fact differ in three important respects. The first concerns the way in which the nervous typological basis of personality is conceptualized. According to Eysenck each personality dimension has underlying it a separate psychophysiological process which varies independently and the strength of which determines the individual's position on the appropriate dimension. By contrast, the present model proposed that the personality dimensions actually arise through a difference in the way in which the *same* set of physiological mechanisms interact. The crucial emphasis here, therefore, is on the *organization* of nervous typological processes as the essential feature distinguishing personality variations.

The second distinction between the two theories concerns the usage of the terms "neuroticism" and "psychoticism". According to Eysenck the latter, together with introversion–extraversion, refer to three quite independent personality dimensions, variations along one being un-influenced by variations along another. As viewed, here, however, neuroticism and psychoticism would cut across the dimensional structure of personality described by Eysenck. This proposal has two consequences. One is that variations in characteristics associated with introversion–extraversion are considered to be very closely dependent on an individual's weighting on neuroticism or psychoticism, in the sense that the latter two dimensions will determine different aspects of extraversion, as shown in Fig. 6.1. The second consequence is that the questionnaire scales of neuroticism and psychoticism developed by Eysenck do not line up exactly with the equivalent dimensions post-ulated here. This has become particularly evident following the study reported by Claridge and Chappa (to appear) and described briefly in the previous chapter. Those authors, it will be recalled, found that the nervous typological organization of individuals with low scores on one of Eysenck's neuroticism scales was similar to that observed in psychotic states and in subjects selected, on the basis of a questionnaire, as being high on psychoticism. Claridge and Chappa considered that low neuroticism, as measured by Eysenck, actually represents a form of psychoticism, namely that associated with the retarded end of the di-mension described by Claridge. It is clear, then, that at the descriptive level the theory of Eysenck and that proposed by the present author do not coincide.

A third and more general difference between the two models is that that discussed here has been developed more directly from research on the extreme forms of nervous typological variation observed in psy-chiatric groups. This strategy has allowed both the descriptive and the biological characteristics of neuroticism and psychoticism to be defined more adequately. However, it has resulted in less attention being paid to normal personality differences, a deficiency it was hoped to remedy in the present study by analyzing the twin data from a similar nervous typological standpoint. In doing so we had three main aims in view. The first was to determine whether the two components of psychophysiological activity previously found, namely tonic arousal and arousal modulation, could also be demonstrated on a group of psychiatrically well individuals. If so we, secondly, wished to discover whether the relationships between variations on these components and personality were in line with the original model. Thirdly, we were interested in examining the model from a genetic point of view by making comparisons, on appropriate parameters, between MZ and DZ twin pairs in the sample. Each of these parts of the analysis will be considered in turn in the section below.

Testing the model

Principal components analysis of the data

The first step in testing the model was undertaken by carrying out a principal components analysis on a relevant set of psychophysiological measures taken from the twin project. The variables chosen for analysis were selected as being broadly similar to those used in the original study of psychiatric patients. As shown in Table 6.1, they included three

TABLE 6.1
VARIABLES ENTERED INTO PRINCIPAL
COMPONENTS ANALYSIS

1	Alpha index at rest
2	Mean alpha frequency
3	Mean alpha blocking
4	Two-flash threshold
5	Spiral after-effect
6	Skin potential level
7	Skin potential orienting response
8	Skin potential cold pressor response
9	Skin potential cold pressor recovery time
10	Skin potential spontaneous fluctuations at rest
11	Heart rate level at rest
12	Sedation threshold

EEG and two perceptual measures, six autonomic indices, and the sedation threshold. With the exception of the latter, which was described in the previous chapter, the experimental procedures involved in obtaining each of the measures have been detailed by Dr Hume in Chapter 4. Inclusion of the sedation threshold as a variable necessarily limited the size of the sample available, but it was considered vital to enter that measure into the analysis because of the major role it had played in the development of the theory to be tested here. Of the twenty-one twin pairs to whom the sedation threshold had been administered one was lost because of missing data on other variables. The sample used for the present analysis therefore consisted of forty subjects, made up of ten sets of MZ and ten sets of DZ twins.

Twelve factors were extracted from the principal components analysis but only the first three, or at most four, were considered meaningful. These four were then rotated to a Varimax solution, the appropriate loadings for the twelve variables being given in Table 6.2. The first component shown there is made up largely of the sedation threshold and heart rate level. It is therefore very similar to that found in our earlier analyses and would seem to qualify for the same description

TABLE 6.2
VARIMAX LOADINGS FOR FOUR PRINCIPAL COMPONENTS

	1	2	3	4
1 Alpha index	+0·16	+0·79	−0·29	−0·21
2 Alpha frequency	+0·24	−0·82	−0·26	−0·05
3 Alpha blocking	+0·03	−0·49	+0·74	−0·05
4 TFT	−0·11	+0·06	+0·01	−0·75
5 SAE	+0·31	+0·42	+0·09	+0·56
6 SP level	+0·11	−0·06	+0·41	+0·27
7 SP orienting response	−0·48	−0·46	−0·03	+0·47
8 SP CP response	−0·01	−0·16	+0·32	+0·48
9 SP CP recovery time	+0·37	+0·09	+0·58	+0·32
10 SP spontaneous fluctuations	+0·14	−0·29	−0·77	+0·08
11 Heart rate	+0·82	−0·07	−0·08	+0·33
12 Sedation threshold	+0·78	0·00	+0·11	+0·01
Latent root	1·86	2·06	1·93	1·68

of "tonic arousal". It is interesting to note that the skin potential orienting response has a *negative* loading on the factor, perhaps reflecting an influence of the law of initial values on this measure of autonomic reactivity. The second factor consists principally of EEG parameters, with very high loadings on alpha index and alpha frequency and a somewhat smaller one on the alpha-blocking response. Two other measures associated with this factor are the skin potential orienting response and the spiral after-effect which somewhat unexpectedly is loaded negatively. Apart from that anomaly, however, the factor would correspond closely to that identified in our earlier study as "arousal modulation".

Factor 3 seems to be mainly loaded on skin potential measures, though it does have a high loading on the alpha-blocking response. The direction and pattern of loadings here suggest a factor in which a marked EEG response to visual stimulation, slow recovery to autonomic stress, and diminished frequency of spontaneous skin potential fluctuations are associated. It is possible that this factor represents some aspect of cortical–subcortical relationships, perhaps concerned with feedback control mechanisms linking EEG and autonomic activity. In that case it may reflect one of the functions previously assigned to "arousal modulation" and illustrated earlier in Fig. 6.2; namely that of facilitation and inhibition of tonic arousal. Factor 2 would then presumably be more narrowly associated with that aspect of arousal modulation concerned with the regulation of sensory input. However, this is purely speculative and it must be admitted that Factor 3 cannot be interpreted with any certainty. The same is true of Factor 4 which, apart from moderate loadings on two of the skin potential measures, the orienting and cold pressor responses, is mainly weighted on the spiral after-effect and two-flash threshold. The pattern of loadings suggests a factor of "perceptual responsiveness".

Apart from a few minor discrepancies, the results of the analysis carried out on the present data coincide remarkably closely with those obtained on a quite different sample of subjects. As before, there is clear evidence for the existence of the component of psychophysiological activity which we have termed "tonic arousal" and which is defined by the two theoretically important measures of activation, the sedation threshold and heart rate. In addition, a quite separate central nervous component, defined by EEG parameters, again emerges. This component we have named "arousal modulation" and assigned to it certain hypothetical regulating functions. As described earlier, we have also suggested that it is the relative balance between tonic arousal and arousal modulation which accounts for an important part of the biological basis of personality. Having confirmed the existence of the two factors in the psychophysiological data it is now possible to examine their personality correlates.

Nervous typological analysis

The usual approach to research in this area involves selecting individuals of different personality type, either on the basis of psychiatric diagnosis or in terms of personality questionnaire scores, and then comparing them on various measures of psychophysiological response. This was essentially the technique used for analysing the sedation threshold data reported in the previous chapter. A different research strategy, and the one adopted here, is to reverse that procedure and classify subjects into "nervous types" in terms of their behaviour on psychophysiological parameters, then examining how they differ on a number of descriptive characteristics. In this context the term "descriptive" usually refers to personality traits though, as argued in Chapter 1, and as used here, it can be validly extended to cover other sources of behavioural variation, such as cognitive characteristics.

Following the theoretical model of personality already outlined, the subjects in the present study were divided into different nervous types according to their relative weightings on the two factors of "tonic arousal" and "arousal modulation" isolated in the principal components analysis described in the previous section. For each subject two factor scores were calculated, one derived from each component. By dividing the two components at their respective means it was then possible to plot each subject in the two-dimensional space defined by the two factors. The actual distribution of the forty subjects available within this factor space is shown in Fig. 6.3. The four quadrants in that diagram therefore correspond to those shown earlier in Fig. 6.1 and represent different combinations of "tonic arousal" and "arousal modulation" which, it is postulated, are related in a theoretically

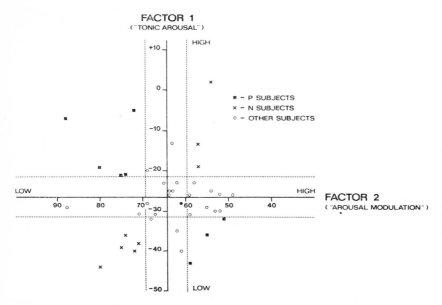

FIG. 6.3. Diagram illustrating procedure used to select "psychotic" nervous types (P subjects) and "neurotic" nervous types (N subjects). Axes, which represent factor scores for the first two principal components, have been drawn so as to facilitate comparison with Fig. 6.1. Broken lines indicate $\frac{1}{2}$ SD limits used to define groups.

meaningful way to the descriptive features of neuroticism and psychoticism. Accordingly, "neuroticism" would run from the top right to the bottom left quadrants and "psychoticism" from the top left to the bottom right quadrants.

For the purpose of the present analysis subjects were chosen whose factor scores placed them clearly in one of the two "neurotic" or one of the two "psychotic" quadrants. As illustrated in Fig. 6.3, this was done by selecting those individuals whose scores on *both* factors placed them outside certain limits, defined by lines drawn half a standard deviation either side of each factor mean. Subjects meeting these criteria and falling in either the top right or bottom left quadrants were considered together as being of "neurotic" nervous type and named the

N group. Conversely, those outside the prescribed limits in the top left and bottom right quadrants were regarded as "psychotic" nervous types and designated the P group. Defined in this way each group contained eight subjects.

Examination of the ways in which these two nervous typological groups differed in descriptive characteristics was carried out by comparing them with respect to a number of personality and cognitive variables. Considering the latter first, and bearing in mind some of the arguments put forward elsewhere in the book, particularly in Chapter 3, the most obvious prediction to be made would be that individuals of "psychotic" nervous type, that is subjects in the P group, would differ in cognitive function. This possibility was tested by comparing the P and N groups on two sets of measure obtained by Mrs Canter, namely scores on divergent thinking tests and on tests of conceptual thinking. With regard to the total divergent thinking, or "creativity", score it was found that the two groups differed significantly. In line with expectation P subjects had a higher score than N subjects, the means being 270·1 (range 119–396) and 181·4 (range 90–269), respectively. Using the Mann–Whitney U test the difference between these distributions was found to be significant at the 0·04 level. Examination of the individual divergent thinking tests indicated that this significant tendency for P subjects to be more creative held up for two of the five measures contributing to the total score, namely the Unusual Uses and Object Drawing tests. The higher scores of P subjects on these two tests were found to be significant at the 0·01 and 0·03 levels of confidence, respectively (Mann–Whitney U test). In evaluating this result it is interesting to note that, in Mrs Canter's own analysis reported in Chapter 3, Unusual Uses and Object Drawing had the lowest correlations with general intelligence; suggesting that variations in performance on them are as, if not more, dependent on personality, and hence nervous typological, differences in cognitive style. This would be confirmed by the finding here that the N and P groups did not differ on either measure of general intelligence available for the subjects.

Turning to the other group of cognitive tests which may be considered relevant—conceptual thinking—it was found that the P group differed from the N group in the expected direction on all four of the main measures taken from that part of the study; though only in one case did the difference reach statistical significance. As would be predicted from the assumption that P subjects were nervous types loaded on psychoticism, they showed more unusual sortings on the Payne Object Classification Test, were more overinclusive on the Chapman II test and less overexclusive on both the Chapman I and Chapman II tests. It was on the last of these that the difference between the groups reached statistical significance ($p < 0.04$, Mann–Whitney U test).

The personality correlates of the nervous typological differences present in the P and N groups were examined with reference to the model described earlier, the predictions made becoming evident by glancing back at Fig. 6.1. Specifically, it was expected that in the two types of subject there would be different relationships between tonic arousal and extraversion, including the latter's component factors, impulsivity and sociability. To test this prediction a series of Spearman rank-order correlations were calculated in each group separately between these three personality measures and two measures of tonic arousal, the sedation threshold and the factor scores derived from Factor 1 of the principal components analysis which had provided the basis for the division into P and N subjects. The measures of impulsivity and sociability used were, of course, derived from the appropriate questionnaire described in Chapter 2; while, as in the previous chapter, a composite score of extraversion was obtained by combining the E-scale of the EPI and the second-order E factor on the 16PF.

Considering total extraversion first, results exactly in line with expectation were found. That is to say, correlations with tonic arousal were opposite in direction in the P group, compared with the N group; though only in one case was statistical significance reached. Factor 1 correlated -0.74 ($p < 0.05$) with extraversion in N subjects, indicating, as predicted, that among "neurotic" nervous types the more tonically aroused the individual the more introverted he tended to be. Using the sedation threshold as an index of tonic arousal the result, while in the same direction, was less clear, *rho* being -0.48 (NS). Among "psychotic" nervous types the tendency was for the more tonically aroused to be more *extraverted*, the correlations with E being $+0.50$ (NS) for the Factor 1 measure and $+0.38$ (NS) for the sedation threshold.

As might be expected, the findings for the two components of extraversion paralleled the above results, though in the P group the pattern of correlations was again less clear-cut. There the correlations between sociability and the two tonic arousal measures were very low, being $+0\cdot12$ for the factor score index and $+0\cdot08$ for the sedation threshold. The equivalent correlations with impulsivity were somewhat higher, being $+0\cdot50$ (NS) and $+0\cdot54$ (NS), respectively. By contrast, in the N group there was a strong tendency for impulsivity to be *negatively* related to tonic arousal, at least as measured by the factor score, *rho* being $-0\cdot88$ ($p<0\cdot01$). Using the sedation threshold the correlation was still negative but much lower (*rho* $= -0\cdot33$, NS). These negative correlations in the N group also held up for sociability but neither *rho* value was significant, being $-0\cdot50$ in the case of the factor score and $-0\cdot37$ in the case of the sedation threshold.

To summarize the results in this section, it may be said that, although many of the statistics failed to reach significance, all of the trends were in the theoretically expected direction and therefore provided some validity for the method used of sub-dividing the subjects in terms of their psychophysiological status. Individuals who, in nervous type, can be identified as being similar to psychotic patients and who may, therefore, be said to be loaded on a dimension of psychoticism, show a predictable pattern of performance on cognitive tests chosen because of their theoretical relevance as measures of thinking styles known to be associated with psychosis. Furthermore, such individuals tend to show a personality structure, in terms of extraversion, which is predictable from the model described earlier and which was itself based on the study of psychiatric patients. Thus, among P subjects, as we have called them here, tonic arousal tends to be higher in extraverts, a finding incidentally directly confirming a similar result previously obtained in diagnosed psychotics (Claridge, 1967). "Neurotic" nervous types, again selected according to their psychophysiological similarity to neurotic patients, also show a personality structure predictable from the model, the more aroused individuals here being, in contrast to "psychotic" types, *less* extraverted and impulsive.

It is of interest to compare the results reported here with those described in the previous chapter where a different research strategy was used; that is, subjects were subdivided in terms of questionnaire scores rather than on the basis of nervous typological criteria. In fact, the two sets of data are remarkably consistent with each other. Thus, the relationships between measures of tonic arousal and extraversion found here among "neurotic" nervous types exactly parallel those found in the previous chapter among subjects with high questionnaire neuroticism scores. The opposite relationships observed there between sedation threshold and extraversion among *low* N-scorers is also theoretically in line with the similar result obtained here in "psychotic" nervous types, in view of the independent evidence already quoted that individuals high on psychoticism and those low in neuroticism share a similar psychophysiological make-up (Claridge and Chappa, to appear).

Finally, it should be stressed that the number of subjects on which the present study was based was small and the strength of the results lies in their theoretical consistency rather than in sample size. Given this proviso, the findings do suggest a possible fruitful area for research, using similar techniques, in order to establish in more detail the variations in nervous typological organization associated with different kinds of personality structure.

MZ/DZ comparisons

The third, and final, aspect of the results to be considered here concerns the extent to which the data provide evidence for genetic determination of the psychophysiological parameters on which the nervous typological analysis was based. This was done by calculating, in the MZ and DZ twin pairs making up the sample, intraclass correlations for the factor scores derived from each of the four factors of the principal components analysis described earlier. It will be recalled that the number of twins of each type was ten.

The most striking finding here concerned Factor 2 which was made up largely of EEG measures and which we identified as being similar to that described in our previous work as "arousal modulation". The intraclass correlations for MZ and DZ twins on this factor were, respectively, $+0.96\,(p<0.001)$ and $+0.54\,(p<0.05)$. In other words, the values for r_1 closely approached those expected from the hypothesis of complete genetic determination and certainly suggest a strong hereditary influence on this EEG factor.

The other main psychophysiological component with which we have been concerned here, "tonic arousal", represented by Factor 1, revealed little evidence of genetic determination. Indeed, the intraclass correlation was somewhat higher in DZ twins ($+0.61$, $p < 0.05$) than in MZ twins ($+0.41$, NS). This finding contrasts somewhat with that for the sedation threshold which of course contributed strongly to Factor 1 and which, as will be recalled from the previous chapter, did appear to be significantly influenced by genetic factors, even though two MZ twin pairs were very discordant on the test. Clearly, some of the variance on the sedation threshold attributable to heredity is lost when the measure is included as a part of a composite index of psychophysiological activity. This may be because some of the other measures determining Factor 1, such as heart rate, are so transient in character.

Of the other two factors extracted from the principal components analysis neither showed a clear-cut difference between MZ and DZ twins. On Factor 3, a factor mainly loaded on skin potential variables, DZ pairs were again somewhat more alike than MZ pairs, though in neither case was the intraclass correlation significant, the values for r_1 being $+0.40$ and $+0.20$, respectively. For the fourth factor, tentatively identified as being concerned with perceptual function, the intraclass correlations were virtually the same in the two types of twin, being $+0.39$ (NS) for MZ and $+0.34$ (NS) for DZ pairs.

Discussion and conclusions

The purpose of this chapter has been to try and integrate some of the findings from other parts of the study. This has been done from a relatively narrowly defined theoretical viewpoint and inevitably large areas of the data gathered on our twin sample have been ignored. However, as far as it went, the analysis reported here produced encouraging results, vindicating both the methodological approach used and the theoretical framework within which it was undertaken. Factor analysis of the psychophysiological data confirmed previous work of a similar kind in demonstrating the existence of two components which could be used in a meaningful way as a basis for the nervous typological classification of normal subjects, in whom predictable differences in personality and cognitive function were shown to exist. Thus, different combinations of what we have termed "tonic arousal" and "arousal modulation" seem to define two personality dimensions which previous research on the appropriate psychiatric criterion groups has identified as neuroticism and psychoticism, respectively. The latter dimension would seem, at the nervous typological level, to be represented by a relative "dissociation" between tonic arousal and arousal modulation, high levels in one system being accompanied by low levels in the other. A different kind of nervous typological organization in which both systems are congruent in their activity, would seem, from this and our previously reported evidence, to be identifiable at the descriptive level as neuroticism. As predicted from the original model, the psychophysiological basis of extraversion appears to be a complex interaction between these two dimensions, its correlations with nervous typological measures depending on whether the individual is loaded on psychoticism or on neuroticism.

In evaluating the above conclusions it is of interest to compare the results reported here with those described in Chapter 4 by Dr Hume who also carried out a principal components analysis of the psychophysiological data, though on a larger set of variables. As Dr Hume points out, the results of his analysis do not coincide entirely with those of the present study, which was confined to subjects on whom the edation threshold was available. He suggests quite rightly that the satter individuals were not representative of the twin sample as a whole, In the sense that self-selection for undergoing the sedation threshold inevitably introduced some bias, as did the age limit we ourselves imposed. A more crucial question, however, concerns the representativeness and theoretical relevance of the variables chosen for consideration in the two analyses. As the results subsequently confirmed, the present study had the advantage of being anchored at all points to existing theory rather than relying on the exploration of relationships between variables chosen on a purely empirical basis.

From the genetic point of view the most interesting finding here was the very positive evidence in favour of "arousal modulation" being strongly influenced by heredity. This fact suggests that the cortical regulating and attentional control functions referred to arousal modulation may play the primary biological role in determining nervous typological differences, the other psychophysiological systems involved, such as "tonic arousal", perhaps being secondarily influenced by it and subject to considerable environmental modification. This possibility might partly answer a question posed by the present author in a previous discussion of his model, as to which part of the feedback link between tonic arousal and arousal modulation is primarily "dissociated" in psychotic disturbance (Claridge, 1967). It might also have some implications for the further understanding of the genetic basis of psychosis, in which disorders of attention, rather than of arousal as such, appear to predominate.

References

CLARIDGE, G. S. (1967) *Personality and Arousal.* Pergamon, Oxford.

CLARIDGE, G. S. and CHAPPA, H. J. Psychoticism: a study of its biological basis in To appear in normal subjects. *Brit. J. soc. clin. Psychol.*

EYSENCK, H. J. (1957) *Dynamics of Anxiety and Hysteria.* Routledge and Kegan Paul, London.

CHAPTER 7

AN IDIOGRAPHIC ANALYSIS OF DIFFERENCES BETWEEN SOME DISCORDANT MZ TWIN PAIRS

By GORDON CLARIDGE

Introduction

In Chapter 1 it was noted that a potentially useful variation on the usual group comparison approach to twin research is the detailed examination of individual pairs, particularly monozygotic pairs, discordant for some important characteristic. The study of other ways in which such twins differ should help to throw light on the mechanisms which have led to their discordance on the characteristic in question. Ideally, of course, an investigation of that kind should be prospective in nature, following through twins found to be different early in life. However, even the less powerful approach of looking at correlated areas of dissimilarity in adult pairs has some value since it may lead to hypotheses that can be tested by prospective research.

Our own interest in looking at the present twin sample from this idiographic viewpoint arose originally out of our involvement in trying to explain the discordance observed on the sedation threshold, described in Chapter 5. There, it will be recalled, we were able in one discordant pair to suggest a number of alternative hypotheses to explain their dissimilarity in barbiturate tolerance. This led us to search through our records for other MZ pairs who were markedly discordant on other characteristics we had measured. Our hope was that some of these pairs would differ in several ways which, taken together, would be meaningful when judged against the theoretical background of the project as a whole. At the outset we were aware that the conclusions we were likely to reach would probably be very limited and rather tentative. Nevertheless, we considered the study worth undertaking and reporting here, if only as an illustrative exercise in methodology.

Selection of discordant pairs

In order to identify twin pairs who were sufficiently different for them to be considered discordant in anything other than a trivial sense it was first necessary to decide upon some criteria for dissimilarity. As an

TABLE 7.1
MEASURES USED FOR SELECTING DISCORDANT TWIN PAIRS

Group	Test	Measure
Personality	EPI EPI Sociability/Impulsivity Scale Sociability/Impulsivity Scale 16PF 16PF 16PF	E-score N-score Impulsivity score Sociability score Second-order E-score Second-order A-score Second-order N-score
General cognitive	Creativity tests Creativity tests Creativity tests Creativity tests Creativity tests Creativity tests Progressive Matrices Mill Hill Vocabulary Scale	Word Association score Unusual Uses score Object Drawing score Consequences score Gottschaldt Figures score Total score Percentile score Percentile score
Conceptual	Object Classification Test Chapman Test I Chapman Test II Chapman Test II	Non-A score Total score Overinclusion score Overexclusion score
Physiological	Factor score—1 Factor score—2 Factor score—3 Factor score—4 Factor score—5	Autonomic level score Sympathetic responsiveness score EEG arousal score Spontaneous GSR activity score Perceptual function score

initial screening procedure two basic criteria were adopted. The first required that the members of a given pair differed to a degree which was equal to at least one standard deviation from the mean MZ intra-pair difference score on a particular measure. The second was that this first criterion must be met on at least two measures of the same type. For the latter purpose the measures included as a basis for selection were considered under four headings, shown in Table 7.1. It will be seen there that only certain tests or experimental procedures, and only certain scores derived from them, were used. This was because it was considered desirable to confine ourselves to those measures which were most stable or of greatest theoretical interest. Thus, in the case of the personality tests we excluded the Foulds Hostility Scale and the first-order factor scores of the 16PF. However, any discordance occurring on those measures was recorded on the twins who met our criteria for dissimilarity on the four main test groups. Another point to note in Table 7.1 is that the selection for discordance on the physiological measures was based on factor scores derived from the principal components analysis of these data reported by Dr Hume in Chapter 4.

Using the criteria just described we identified sixteen pairs of monozygotic twins who were discordant on at least one group of measures. These pairs could be further subdivided into three categories, according to their degree of discordance and the amount of additional information available on them. The categories were as follows:

1. Those who were discordant on *more than one* of the four groups of measure. Here there were *four pairs*, three of whom differed by one SD or more on several measures other than those on which they met the criteria for discordance.
2. Those who were discordant on *one* group only. *Six pairs* were found here, all of them differing by one SD or more on measures other than those on which they met the criteria for discordance.
3. Those who were discordant on *one* group only, but showed no marked differences on any other measures. *Six pairs* fell into this category.

Since the success of the enquiry depended on our being able to correlate across differences observed on several types of measure the six pairs falling into the last category were of little interest and will not be considered further here; except to record that five of the pairs were discordant on the personality, and one pair on the creativity, tests.

Inspection of the data for the six twins falling into the second category indicated that here, too, there was little that warranted extensive comment and these pairs will not be described in detail either. Three of the pairs were discordant on the physiological measures and also showed some differences on the personality tests. Of the remaining three pairs in this category two were discordant in creativity and differed on one of the physiological factors; while the other pair met the criteria for discordance on the personality tests and showed a minor difference in conceptual thinking.

Description of four discordant pairs

Having eliminated for detailed consideration those sets of twins who were discordant on less than two of the major groups of measure described in the previous section, four pairs remained. Here an attempt will be made to draw together some of the areas of discordance observed in these pairs. In doing so, in order to preserve anonymity the pairs will be referred to by number and the individual members as A and B. Details of the measures on which each of the four sets of twins differed, together with age, sex, and years of separation, are given in Table 7.2. A general point to note there is that three of the four twins were older than the average age for the sample as a whole, while only one of the pairs was still unseparated.

Of the twins shown in Table 7.2, Pair One provided most room for interpretation of their discordance. Twin A was a professional artist, his brother a student of East European languages. A showed a higher level of EEG arousal and, consistent with this, emerged on the personality tests as more highly driven in several respects. He had greater anxiety/neuroticism on the EPI N-scale and Q4 factor of the 16PF and showed more hostility as measured by the Foulds questionnaire. Because the nature of physiological Factor 5 is not entirely clear (see Chapter 4) the pair's discordance here is less easy to interpret, though it is of interest in view of the consistency with which it appeared in some of the other twins discussed below. The factor seems to be one of perceptual function, the direction of discordance in Pair One, in terms

TABLE 7.2
DETAILS OF FOUR DISCORDANT PAIRS

Pair number	Sex	Age	Discordance Group	Discordance Measure	Other differences
One	M	35	Physiological	Factors 3 and 5	Conceptual: Chapman II overinclusive score
			General Cognitive	Progressive Matrices Creativity: Consequences, Gottschaldt Figures	
Two	F	34	Physiological	Factors 1, 4 and 5	Personality: Impulsivity, 16PF first-order N and Q2, Foulds DH score
			General Cognitive Conceptual	Creativity: Total score, Object Drawing Chapman II overexclusion score Payne OCT Non-A score	
Three	F	22	Physiological	Factors 1 and 5	Personality: 16PF first-order Q3 and Q4, Foulds DG score
			General Cognitive	Mill Hill Vocabulary Creativity: Total score, Object Drawing	
Four	F	39	General Cognitive Personality	Creativity: Unusual Uses, Object Drawing 16PF second-order A and N	

of the individual measures loading on it, indicating a shorter spiral after-effect and higher two-flash threshold in Twin A. It is possible, and this is supported by other findings described later, that the difference between the pair members on Factor 5 is in some way relevant to their discordance on the creativity tests, reflecting some aspects of a relationship between divergent thinking and certain features of attention, such as scanning, as discussed by Mrs Canter in Chapter 3. Certainly eyemovements, the physical counterpart of scanning, have been implicated in the spiral after-effect (Holland, 1965), a fact which might provide some rationale for linking the two areas of psychological function together.

On the creativity tests themselves Twin A, the artist, predictably emerged with higher scores and, theoretically in line with this, was also more overinclusive on one of the conceptual tests. Surprisingly, he also had a much lower Progressive Matrices score, falling at the 50th percentile only, as against the 90th percentile reached by his brother. Both twins, however, showed equally high verbal ability as measured by the Mill Hill Vocabulary Scale. Twin A's poorer Matrices score may in some way be connected with his greater tendency to divergent thinking. As a test the Progressive Matrices capitalizes considerably on the ability to think in a convergent manner, the subject being required to seek one correct solution to each problem from among several offered alternatives. It might be argued that the extremely divergent and overinclusive thinker, as Twin A appeared to be, is handicapped in that sort of test situation, attempting to find unusual, though to him, equally correct, solutions. The result is in any case of general interest in view of the findings reported in Chapter 3; namely the very positive correlation between intelligence and creativity test performance observed in the group as a whole and the tendency for this relationship to break down at high levels of IQ.

One further difference between the members of Pair One that should be mentioned is the fact that one of twins (B) suffered from diabetes mellitus, apparently having developed the condition following a period of stress. The aetiology of diabetes mellitus is extremely complex but both genetic and exogenous factors have been implicated. As far as the former are concerned it apparently shows some close parallels with psychological conditions where graded degrees of genetic predisposition suggest multifactorial inheritance (Gottesman and Shields, 1968). With regard to external precipitants the psychosomatic aspects of the disorder have been widely discussed (Lidz, 1954). It is not inconceivable, therefore, that the development of diabetes in the more self-controlled Twin B represented his tendency to somaticize anxiety for which his brother found expression in more overt behaviour through externalization of effect in artistic pursuits.

Of the four twins under consideration Pair Two showed the greatest degree of discordance as judged by the number of major test groups of which they differed: physiological, conceptual, and general cognitive. The pattern of discordance was also remarkably similar to that found in Pair One. Thus, the more creative Twin A was again more overinclusive on one of the conceptual tests. Consistent with this she was also less *overexclusive* on another. Physiologically A also differed from her twin on the perceptual Factor 5 in the same direction as that shown by the more creative member of Pair One; that is, she showed low spiral after-effect and high two-flash threshold. The more creative Twin A was also more aroused, though unlike Pair One the difference here appeared on the autonomic factors (1 and 4), rather than on the EEG factor. The personality differences found for this pair indicated that Twin A was less impulsive and intropunitive and on the 16PF more self-sufficient and shrewd.

The tendency for the direction of discordance on the divergent thinking and physiological measures to show a certain degree of consistency was further upheld in Pair Three. Here the more creative twin was again more autonomically aroused—on Factor 1—and again differed in perceptual function (Factor 5) in the same direction as the previous pairs. Another noticeable difference in this pair occurred on the Mill Hill Vocabulary Scale, the more creative twin having a higher verbal IQ. In personality she was more tense and more hostile.

Unfortunately, no physiological data were available for Pair Four and therefore it was not possible to check the relationships observed above between creativity and physiological status. However, it is worth noting that findings consistent with these relationships were observed in two of the pairs rejected for detailed discussion here because they were discordant on only one major test group, namely the two sets of twins in category 2 who differed on the creativity measures. In one of these cases the more creative member showed higher EEG arousal. In the other case it was the perceptual factor that differentiated the twins, the more divergent thinking again showing a score indicative of a low spiral after-effect and a high two-flash threshold.

Returning briefly to Pair Four, the only other way in which they were discordant, that is apart from creativity, was in personality, the more divergent thinking twin being less anxious and neurotic as measured by the 16PF-second-order factors. This was in keeping with the general finding reported by Mrs Canter in Chapter 3 that creativity test performance was negatively correlated with anxiety/neuroticism; though the result was not consistently confirmed in the other discordant pairs.

General conclusions

As anticipated at the beginning of this chapter, only limited conclusions could be drawn about the individual sets of twins considered here. Mainly it has been possible only to comment on some of the correlated areas of discordance, looking at these against the background of results reported in earlier chapters. However, one finding suggesting a possible area for further research was the consistent relationship, observed across five discordant twin pairs, between differences in thinking style, on the one hand, and physiological status, on the other. Of particular interest was the finding that in all five pairs the most creative twin differed in the same direction on the physiological factor of perceptual function, a factor which we suggested may highlight individual variations in attention mode. The tendency for differences in creativity to be partly related to nervous typological organization in a general sense has already been discussed in Chapter 6, where some experimental evidence in line with that hypothesis was presented. Looked at from the different, idiographic, viewpoint adopted in this chapter some further support for this possibility has been found, though the nature of the present result is such that it can only be regarded as a pointer towards an area of cognition research which might be worth exploring further.

An obvious weakness of the present study has been our inability to throw light, with the possible exception of Pair One, on the mechanisms leading to discordance in the twins described. This is not surprising in view of the retrospective nature of the enquiry. Another difficulty is that we have been dealing with a series of characteristics which, as judged by the results reported in the previous chapters, are subject to differing degrees of genetic control. Even on those traits, such as creativity, which have a significant hereditary component, there is clearly considerable room for environmental modification leading, in some MZ pairs, to the marked degree of discordance defined here. On the other hand, it is of some interest that so few really discordant pairs were identified, even on variables which the group comparison data suggested were determined as much by environmental as by genetic factors. This at least must force us to the conclusion that when their behaviour is sampled on a very wide variety of measures, monozygotic twins are remarkably similar at the phenotypic level.

References

GOTTESMAN, I. I. and SHIELDS, J. (1968) In pursuit of the schizophrenic genotype. In Vandenberg, S. G. (Ed.) *Progress in Human Behaviour Genetics.* Johns Hopkins Press, Baltimore.

HOLLAND, H. C. (1965) *The Spiral After-effect.* Pergamon, Oxford.

LIDZ, T. (1954) Psychological aspects of diabetes mellitus. In Wittkower, E. D. and Cleghorn, R. A. (Eds.) *Recent Advances in Psychosomatic Medicine.* Pitman London.

CHAPTER 8

FINAL REMARKS

By GORDON CLARIDGE

THE approach to individual variation adopted in this book has had three characteristic features. It has been nomothetic, it has laid stress on the psychophysiological basis of behaviour, and it has explicitly recognized the contribution of heredity to human differences. Logically, of course, no one of these features implies either of the other two. It is perfectly possible to have a nomothetic model of personality without reference to biological data; while the relative roles of genetic and environmental factors in behaviour can be given varying degrees of emphasis, whatever one's theoretical standpoint on other issues. In practice, however, opposing views of the three modes of explanation have tended to cluster together, the position taken here contrasting with that of the more socially orientated idiographist seeking to account for behaviour in terms of purely psychological constructs. In trying to draw some general conclusions from the studies described in the previous chapters I am aware that, because of the whims of fashion, I am now writing in a climate of opinion that is largely unreceptive to the kind of facts my colleagues and I have reported. Social, educational, and political thinking is currently being carried along on a wave of environmentalism which, while paying lip-service to the fact that one reason why people differ is because they vary in genetic make-up, in reality ignores it. On the narrower front of abnormal psychology, but reflecting the same trend, the analysis of individual variation using conventional experimental techniques has tended to recede of late, giving way to more person-centred formulations which, while factually less substantial, are seen as having greater immediate relevance to social and clinical problems.

This swing in the pendulum of psychological theorizing represents a general rejection of the applicability of traditional scientific methods to the study of human differences which the emphasis on the nomothetic and the biological implies. However, in a more specific sense, it is also partly due to the slow rate at which progress has been made in discovering universal laws of personality and in establishing their biological basis. Thus, it must be admitted that the early hopes of constructing a watertight nervous typological theory of individual differences have not yet been fulfilled. Even Professor Eysenck, pioneer of the approach in this country, concedes in his book, *The Biological Basis of Personality*, that the subject matter is more complex that he was once prepared to admit and presents his own revised theory with an uncharacteristic air of uncertainty. Those of us who, in one guise or another, have stayed the course with Eysenck share this uncertainty but believe that with patience it will eventually be possible to tease out the facts of nervous typological organization which provide a biological substrate for personality. As some of the results described in this book illustrate, I think, progress is being made towards that end, even if it is the progress of the tortoise, temporarily overtaken by the more personable hare.

If I had to hazard a guess at where the growing-points will be in future nervous typological research, I would select one as likely to be of particular importance. That is the detailed exploration of psychoticism as a set of normal personality characteristics having definable nervous typological correlates. Several considerations lead me to this conclusion. Eysenck himself is already actively involved in devising questionnaire measures of psychoticism (Eysenck and Eysenck, 1968). Unfortunately these were developed too late for inclusion in the present study; though here, working within a slightly different theoretical model, we have been able to present evidence, supported by results obtained in other parts of our research programme, for psychoticism as a personality dimension. Elsewhere in this book and in a slightly different context—the study of cognitive function—we have seen the possibility of extending the descriptive measurement of psychoticism into the area of thinking, to be linked, via attentional models, to psychophysiological parameters. All of these research developments are occurring against a background of disillusionment with disease views of the psychotic disorders (Claridge, 1972). At present the popular alternatives are couched in the language of interpersonal psychology, but once the more extreme of these views has exhausted its adherents I suspect that nervous typological theory may emerge as a very viable model for describing and understanding a group of personality reactions whose biological flavour is more evident than most.

Turning to the other major area of emphasis here, namely on the genetic basis of individual differences, the opportunity to investigate this aspect of biological variation flowed naturally of course from the fact that our subjects were twins. In reaching conclusions from this part of the study I am aware, as was stressed several times in the book, that from a psychogenetic point of view the particular methodology we were able to use is of limited value. Thus, it has allowed us only to make rather general statements about the relative significance of heredity in determining particular kinds of individual variation and has not enabled us to explore in more detail the exact genetic mechanisms involved or the extent to which hereditary and environmental processes interact. However, for those readers who have come to the book primarily as psychogeneticists the twin data presented may be of interest in drawing attention to parameters of behaviour which might be worth investigating further using more sophisticated research techniques. In this respect the behavioural aspects of drug response might be singled out as a relatively unexplored, but promising, area for further study. Measurement at the nervous typological level generally appeared to provide the clearest evidence of the influence of heredity; though there were two notable exceptions where descriptive measures revealed a significant genetic component. One was extraversion, that is once the effect of twin interaction—an interesting phenomenon in its own right—had been controlled for. The other concerned certain aspects of cognitive function where the important contribution of genetic factors was again confirmed.

The fact that heredity does appear to contribute in varying degrees, and sometimes substantially, to human differences should not need reiterating for, as Mittler (1971) comments (referring to intelligence though his remarks apply equally well to other kinds of individual variation) ". . . there is no reason why man should mark a sharp discontinuity in evolution, and turn out to be totally immune from the workings of genetic processes which affect lower organisms". It is equally difficult to conceive of man's behaviour—including its varieties —being uninfluenced by the broader biological background of which genetic processes form only part. Indeed, the results reported in this volume, while certainly complex and sometimes contradictory, do confirm that biological factors, defined in their widest sense, are partly responsible for personality differences. It therefore follows that any account of variations in human behaviour which does not take account of such factors is necessarily incomplete.

References

CLARIDGE, G. S. (1972) The schizophrenias as nervous types. *Brit. J. Psychiat.* **121**, 1–17.

EYSENCK, H. J. (1967) *The Biological Basis of Personality*. Charles C. Thomas, Springfield, Ill.

EYSENCK, H. J. and EYSENCK, S. B. G. (1968) The measurement of psychoticism: a study of factor stability and reliability. *Brit. J. soc. clin. Psychol.* **7**, 286–94.

MITTLER, P. (1971) *The Study of Twins*. Penguin, London.

APPENDIX 1

DETAILS OF PHYSICAL
RESEMBLANCE QUESTIONNAIRE

As mentioned in Chapter 1, the opportunity was taken during the twin study to construct and administer a questionnaire concerned with physical resemblance; the purpose being to determine whether it would be possible to use such a questionnaire for deciding the zygosity of twin pairs in future, postal, studies. The availability of objective zygosity data, determined by the methods outlined in Chapter 1, allowed us to validate the questionnaire, the format of which is given below.

Physical Resemblance Questionnaire

Below are a number of questions designed to find out the physical similarity between you and your twin. Please answer each question as accurately as possible. Where several alternatives are given put a circle round the answer which most closely applies to you.

1. (a) How would you describe the *natural* colour of your hair?
   black/dark-brown/mid-brown/light-brown/red/blonde
   (b) How does it compare with that of your twin?
   exactly the same/slightly different/very different
2. (a) How would you describe the texture of your hair?
   course/medium/fine
   (b) How does it compare with that of your twin?
   exactly the same/slightly different/very different
3. (a) How would you describe the curliness of your hair?
   very curly/wavy/straight
   (b) How does it compare with that of your twin?
   exactly the same/slightly different/very different

163

4. What is your weight (in stones and pounds)?

5. What is your height (in feet and inches)?

6. (a) *As a child* how often did *your parents* mistake you and your twin for each other?

   frequently/occasionally/rarely/never

   (b) *As a child* how often did *your teacher* mistake you and your twin for each other?

   frequently/occasionally/rarely/never

   (c) *Nowadays* how often do the following people mistake you and your twin for each other?

   your parents: frequently/occasionally/rarely/never
   your close friends: frequently/occasionally/rarely/never
   your casual friends: frequently/occasionally/rarely/never

7. Do you and your twin regard yourselves as identical twins?

The scoring method adopted for the questionnaire was as follows. For Questions 1a, 2a and 3a, concerned with a description of hair type, the categories circled by the members of a pair were compared. On each hair characteristic a point was assigned to the pair for every difference in category chosen. Thus, on Question 1a, if both members circled "red" the score for that characteristic was zero; but if one twin circled "red" and the other "mid-brown" a score of two was given. On Questions 1b, 2b and 3b, concerned with judged similarity in hair type, the three possibilities offered—exactly the same, slightly different, and very different—were scored zero, one and two, respectively. The score for the pair on each of these questions was obtained by summing the score of *both* members. Questions 3 and 4 were scored by assigning one point to the pair if their weights differed by 15 pounds or more and their heights by $1\frac{1}{2}$ inches or more. Otherwise a zero score was assigned. The scoring system for the various parts of Question 6 followed the same principle as that adopted for Questions 1b, 2b and 3b; the points assigned ranging from zero, for the "frequently", to three, for the "never", category. Finally, on Question 7 a point was given for the answer "No" and zero for "Yes", the score for the two pair members being added. A total score on the questionnaire for each set of twins was obtained by simply summing the scores for the individual items.

In all, fifty-two pairs of twins completed the questionnaire, thirty of these having previously been judged to be MZ by objective zygosity testing. In both the MZ and DZ samples most of the twins were female, eight in each group being male.

The ability of the physical resemblance questionnaire to discriminate the two types of twin is shown in Fig. A1. It can be seen that the combined samples form a clearly bimodal distribution with virtually no overlap between them. Using as a cut-off point a score of 24 only one set of DZ twins is misclassified as MZ, and only one MZ pair as DZ.

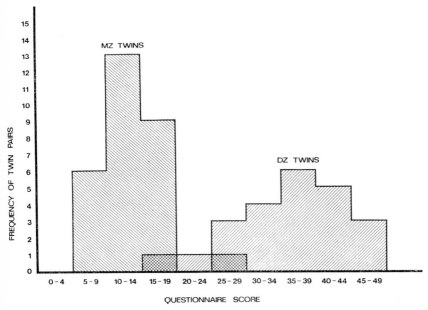

FIG. A1. Frequency distributions of physical resemblance questionnaire scores in MZ twins ($N = 30$) and DZ twins ($N = 22$).

These results provide good validity for the questionnaire and confirm that procedures based on enquiry about superficial physical resemblance may have a place in certain kinds of twin study, where the determination of zygosity by more objective methods is impracticable. However, the cautionary remarks made on this point in Chapter 1 should also be noted, objective zygosity testing being desirable wherever possible.

APPENDIX 2

DETAILS OF OTHER DATA
OBTAINED ON THE TWIN SAMPLE

LISTED below are details of separate studies carried out by other investigators on our twin sample, as well as aspects of our own data not included in this book. In some cases the latter may not be fully analysed but anyone interested in obtaining further information can do so through the people shown, or through Dr Claridge.

1. Similarity in the psychophysiological response of twins to a small dose of chlorpromazine.	Dr G. S. Claridge The University Glasgow
2. Interpersonal perception in twins.	Mr J. Drewery Department of Psychological Research The Crichton Royal Dumfries
3. Semantic differential study of attitudes in twins.	Mrs Sandra Canter c/o Dr. G. S. Claridge The University Glasgow
4. 16PF profile similarity in twins.	Mrs Sandra Canter c/o Dr G. S. Claridge The University Glasgow
5. A biometrical genetical analysis of the data reported in this book.	Dr Lyndon Eaves Department of Genetics The University Edgbaston Birmingham 15

6. Twin similarity in autonomic   Dr W. I. Hume
   response specificity profiles.   University of Leeds
                                        Department of Psychiatry
                                        15 Hyde Terrace
                                        Leeds LS2 9LT

AUTHOR INDEX

SUBJECT INDEX